RAISING
GREAT KIDS
In a Tough World

Susan B. McConnell

PUBLISHING
SINCE 1928

Published by World Publishing, Nashville, TN 37214
www.worldpublishing.com

ISBN: 0-529-12117-4

Printed in the United States of America

2 3 4 5—09 08 07 06 05

DEDICATION

This book is dedicated with love to my husband, Roger, whose love for our children and unselfish attitude exemplifies the unconditional love parents should have for their children.

—*Susan B. McConnell*

TABLE OF CONTENTS

INTRODUCTION

My babies didn't come with an instruction book and Mom was five hundred miles away. Two degrees in psychology weren't much comfort. (I don't recall attending a class on practical parenting skills!) So what was I to do with these seven-pound bundles of joy who came into my life nineteen months apart?

I started studying again! Everything I could read on parenting! I was also blessed to have a good friend who had already become a parent. (Thanks, Deb Beckham Lawson.) Between books, tapes, Bible studies, seminars, mentors, my husband (thanks, Roger for allowing me the privilege of being home with our kids), my mom and mom-in-law (Betty Butler and Louise McConnell, thanks for being great role models), and other family members, I raised two great kids! They are not perfect, of course, because their parents aren't perfect and didn't always make the right decisions raising them. But they are achieving goals in life and possess the foundations to help them become successful.

Children deserve our very best. My hope is that this book will help develop ideas for parenting that will positively impact your family life. The book is divided into five topics: communication, building self-esteem, money matters, discipline, and spiritual training. One book can't give all information needed in raising children. Hopefully, it will provide much needed guidance and spark an interest in learning how to be a positive and effective parent.

PART 1:

BUILDING SELF-ESTEEM IN CHILDREN

CHAPTER 1:

THE IMPORTANCE OF SELF-ESTEEM

Melissa, confident and happy, boarded a jet in Nashville, Tennessee, to return home while Daddy stayed for a week-long meeting. Dressed in her Sunday best and proud of herself for traveling alone, she skipped down the jetway from the airplane to meet her mom who was there to take her home. Quite an experience for a six-year-old, blond-haired, little girl!

This day became one of many "I can do it myself" moments that she filed away in her memory. It gave her another reason to feel good about herself and confident that she was capable of success. Her childhood and teen years offered more of those moments. Time and again she had confidence-building moments because her parents allowed more freedom that produced more success (and sometimes failure) and because her confidence in herself demanded the right to prove herself.

> *Much like a handprint pressed in wet cement, parents imprint children by their words and actions.*

Anne Ortlund's *Children Are Wet Cement* focuses on building self-esteem by encouraging children with positive words and experiences.[1] Much like a handprint pressed in wet cement, parents imprint children by their words and actions. If those words and actions are positive, children will likely develop and mature into confident young adults. Children who grow up with negative words and experiences from parents often lack self-esteem and value. They look at the world as an unfair place to live and feel trapped by circumstances.

Children mirror what parents say and do. Therefore, the parents' attitude and action must reflect what they want them to learn. Parents who themselves grew up in homes that were negative and critical face a particularly difficult challenge. Parents may have to change the image of themselves first and learn to parent in a different way than the way they were raised. But, good news! Parents *can* learn new attitudes about parenting styles even if their own childhood experiences were not the best example.

Parenting is an awesome responsibility for both moms and dads. It requires a *best effort* on the part of both parents—a best effort that may require learning new parenting techniques (which is probably why you're reading this book!).

ROOTS AND WINGS

No one raises perfect kids because no adult is perfect. But we can successfully train happy, confident kids who recognize they are worthwhile. Now that both of my children are away at college or working in a career, it has become clear that giving children roots makes giving them wings easier! When parents are successful in nourishing the roots, children will flap their wings and fly without much help from parents! Just let go and watch them soar!

In preparation for releasing my children from the nest, I wrote each one a book to keep. Each book was composed of three parts: "Before You Were Born," my letters to them during those nine months of expansion and expulsion prior to birth (I was nauseated much of the time); "Special Memories," those fun experiences of childhood from piano recitals to proms; and "Life Instructions," all those things moms tell kids to never forget such as, "He will be just like his dad, so meet the parents," and "You don't have to do everything your crazy friends do!"

As I discussed writing my books with my mom, she said, "Susan, I have a collection of things I have written down over the years that your son Jonathan said to me and prayers he prayed as a child." I laughed and cried as I read through her collection of sweet memories. One humorous story she had recorded was his reason for ceasing to pick his nose at age five. He liked a girl in the fourth grade. Jonathan was afraid that if he picked his nose, the girl's sister, who was in his kindergarten class, would go tell her older sister, whom Jonathan had a crush on! It goes to prove that girls have a special influence on boys—even at a young age!

As I read through Jonathan's prayers, I found that one of them illustrated another essential point. Mom's words:

> "When saying his prayers one night, Jonathan said that his Daddy told him that he loved him so much he would not give anything for him. Jonathan told me he believed his dad really did love him that much."

This is what it is all about. Teaching our kids they are loved and valuable. This is our most important task, along with leading our children to a relationship with Christ. Parents can achieve this by giving children unconditional love just as God loved mankind so much that He gave His only Son to die on the cross for the sins of all people so that all can have eternal life.

LOVING AND ACCEPTING OURSELVES

Is self-esteem biblical? Yes! In God's eyes, we are worth the sacrifice of His Son! If God can love us enough to sacrifice His Son, we should feel comfortable loving and accepting ourselves just as God loves us unconditionally.

Yes, we are sinners, but we are also *forgiven*. We are free to be our best and glorify God as we become all He desires for us. God gives us the power of the resurrection through the Holy Spirit when we allow Him to lead us. In 2 Timothy 1:7 we learn that "God has not given us a spirit of fear, but of power and of love and of a sound mind."

> *If God can love us enough to sacrifice His Son, we should feel comfortable loving and accepting ourselves just as God loves us unconditionally.*

Parents must possess a healthy self-esteem before they are able to help children have a good self-esteem. Self-worth can't be taught by someone who doesn't possess it himself. When we doubt our own self-worth, we should recall that we are created in God's image and have a purpose on earth to multiply and have dominion over the earth (Ge 1:27-28). God made us a little lower than the angels, according to Psalm 8:5. We are worthy in God's eyes because He sacrificed His only Son for our sin (Jo 3:16).

A recent television documentary told the story of a young, pregnant woman who was diagnosed with terminal cancer. The mother-to-be refused chemotherapy treatments because of the harm it could cause to her unborn child. The baby was born healthy, and the mother began treatment following the birth of her daughter. But before the child was two years old, the mother died after battling the cancer. Do you think she had any regrets? Do you think God regrets sacrificing His Son for us? What a touching story of self-sacrificing love.

Because God loved us enough to sacrifice His Son for us, we know we are valuable to Him—so valuable that He sends His angels to watch over us. When the psalmist talks about dwelling in the secret place of the Most High, he says

"For He shall give His angels charge over you, to keep you in all your ways" (Ps 91:11). He loves us so much that He desires a personal relationship with us and will one day be with us forever (Jo 14:1-3). Before teaching a healthy self-esteem to children, we must first know, understand, and believe that we are valuable to God.

SELF-ESTEEM COMES FROM THE HOME

What is self-esteem? It is *not* a noisy, boastful, arrogant attitude that demands attention from the world. A healthy self-esteem is a quiet confidence in one's own self-worth, believing one is valuable and can make a contribution to the world. When one has a healthy self-esteem, he can *give* himself freely to others.

Parents must build self-esteem in children. The world can't do it. Would you trust your child to contemporary society? Do you see a loving, nurturing and protecting world that will encourage your child? Schools can't do it. Schools are overwhelmed with trying to educate children whose parents have failed to develop in them a self-worth that gives confidence and the ability to learn. Churches can't do it either. Churches can reinforce the values parents instill in children, but the time spent at church is not enough for it to be the most influencing factor in building self-esteem.

> *A healthy self-esteem is a quiet confidence in one's own self-worth, believing one is valuable and can make a contribution to the world.*

A child's security comes from the home. It is a refuge for a family to come together and to know love and acceptance. Parents are responsible for providing a nurturing and loving home environment that will train and discipline children. When parents love unconditionally, children will feel self-worth. Parents' love becomes a reference point to understanding God's unconditional love for children.

Self-esteem depends on stability and a nurturing environment in the home. Parents must be committed to their marriage relationship. Having children is the fruit of that relationship. Children need to see the love and respect parents have for each other.

There are unfortunate occasions when it is beyond one's own control to maintain a two parent home. A spouse may die while children are still in the home or may walk out on the marriage relationship. The parental role becomes tougher in single-parent homes, as a parent attempts to provide a stable home environment. As much as it depends on you, as much as it is in your power, make the marriage relationship work. *Your child's ability to love himself and feel loved by others is significantly diminished when a parent walks out of the home and out of the child's life.*

> *To build self-esteem in children, parents must first possess it themselves.*

In private practice, I frequently deal with dysfunctional families where children are experiencing problems because of their parents' divorce. Children will sometimes turn that insecurity inward, withdrawing and displaying anxious feelings. Often there is a lack of motivation to achieve, and sometimes even depression. Insecurity and anger may be turned outward by rebelling against everything and everybody—teachers, parents, and peers. When rebellion occurs, parents may experience a lifetime of heartache and disappointment. A child who has a poor sense of self-worth doesn't see that he can be valuable to the world. He becomes vulnerable to what others think about him and is more likely, as a teen, to join an undesirable peer group that is involved in an immoral or illegal lifestyle.

In summary, to build self-esteem in children, parents must first possess it themselves. Then they must transfer that self-worth to children and (to the best of their ability) must maintain an intact, loving family environment.

CHAPTER 2:

BUILDING SELF-ESTEEM BY ACTIONS

How do we instill self-worth in a child? What *specifically* do parents do to build self-esteem in kids? Showing *unconditional* love and acceptance by actions and attitudes convey value to children. Children can't feel love for themselves if they don't believe they are worthy of love from others.

A story about Benjamin West, a famous British painter, illustrates the impact of a healthy self-worth.[1] As a child, West's mother left her young son to care for his little sister, Sally, while the mother went to the store. While she was gone, Benjamin found some paints, brushes, and paper and began to paint a picture of Sally. When his mother got home, she found that Benjamin had made a mess with the paint. (Can you relate?) Walls, floors, and Benjamin were all covered in paint. But the portrait of Sally was completed. Overlooking the mess he made, Benjamin's mom exclaimed as she looked at the painting, "Why, it's Sally!" Then she stooped down and planted a kiss on Benjamin's forehead. Benjamin West said that his mother's kiss made him a painter. As parents, what would our reaction have been? Would we see the mess or the masterpiece?

It is easier to focus on the mess but always more important to see the art. Parents' reactions to children make lasting impressions in their lives—like wet cement! Be careful to make the right impression because it could stay with your child for a lifetime and will influence how he feels about himself and possibly what he chooses to do in life.

DEMONSTRATING LOVE TO CHILDREN

Children understand love through the quality of relationships with family and caregivers. They feel love by physical touch, eye contact, focused attention, quality time, consistent and fair discipline, and verbal communication. Children need to feel love from parents so that they can appropriately love others and receive love from others. It is very difficult to love another person who does not feel loved or worthwhile. Their personal insecurities make relationships difficult because they do not feel worthy of love and have difficulty trusting others. The most difficult mistake adult children can make is to marry the wrong person. When parents demonstrate a healthy love for each other and transfer that love to children, successful relationships are more probable.

This is especially important for dads with daughters and moms with sons. Children learn about relationships with the opposite sex by first relating to their parent of the opposite sex. A father-daughter relationship that is warm, comfortable, and built on trust will give a girl confidence in relating to young men in a dating relationship. She will not feel threatened or intimidated by them. Her likely choice for a life mate will be a man like dad. If a daughter doesn't grow up with a healthy relationship with dad, she will be more likely to make a poor choice in a marriage partner.

A mother-and-son relationship that is likewise warm, trusting, and open will give a son confidence in relating to young women and showing respect. In the early teen years, begin taking them on "dates." Moms, "date" your son. Dads, "date" your daughters. Take them out alone to dinner, a movie, bowling, or another fun activity. Teach them how to behave on a date. Talk to teens about important aspects in opposite sex relationships, such as mutual respect for one another, trust, consideration, manners, communication, and friendship building. Let them learn the art of dating from you before you send them out with peers.

> *Studies show that physical touch is important to the intellectual and emotional development of children.*

Our son, Jonathan, occasionally took his widowed grandmother out for a date. Grandmother would pick him up, and the two would enjoy an evening together at dinner and a movie. He even split the cost of the date, although Grandmother wanted to pay. Their dates were a special time for building a fun relationship. She always called him "her favorite grandson." No matter that he was her *only* grandson!

IMPORTANCE OF PHYSICAL TOUCH

How do parents show unconditional love? Physical touch, a hug, or a kiss can convey love. Babies need nurturing to thrive and grow. Studies show that physical touch is important to the intellectual and emotional development of children. I guess that's why God sent tiny infants who must be held the first year of life! Even after toddlerhood, children continue to need physical touch. Touching reassures children that they are loved.

Our twenty-something year old daughter still kisses her dad and me when greeting us. (I still kiss my mom, too!) She feels comfortable crawling up in Dad's lap (even in the presence of her "guy" friends). Our son offers hugs to his parents even around his buddies. Children will feel at ease showing affection to parents when they have grown up in homes where physical touch is common.

When hugs and kisses are hard for parents to communicate or when the time is not appropriate, a touch on the shoulder, a tap on the back or arm, or a little nudge will reassure children of parents' love. As children mature, they may resist hugs and kisses around peers, but they still need the reassurance of love. So, when the opportunity is available, at home or elsewhere, show them affection.

Boys respond to wrestling, bear hugs, playful hitting, high fives, and playing games (soccer, basketball) as physical forms of closeness or affection. Girls like to curl up and watch a movie, style one another's hair, paint fingernails, or go shopping!

My husband would occasionally, even through Melissa's teen years, blow dry her hair at night after her shower. (He never offered to blow dry my hair. Go figure!)

Waking children in the morning with a back rub and a kiss provides meaningful physical touch. Sometimes, a parent's best hug is when children are still half asleep in the morning!

Physical touch is one of the five love languages identified by Gary Chapman and Ross Campbell in *The Five Love Languages of Children*.[2] In their book, they identify five love languages that can be used to demonstrate love to another person. The authors identify love languages as physical touch, words of affirmation, quality time, gifts, and acts of service. Every person responds to one or more of these love languages. A person feels love more effectively when others learn to respond to that person in his own love language. Parents effectively can show love to children by learning what love language children respond to and reinforce love with that particular method. (See Chapter 7).

EYE CONTACT

Eye contact is another way to show love. Eye contact tells children that parents are interested in what they are saying or doing. Communication is difficult with someone who is constantly looking away or seems distracted. New parents recognize an infant's need for eye contact within the first few weeks of life. As their eyes begin to focus, they intently watch whoever is holding or caring for them. During feeding times, an infant studies the parent with his eyes and touches him with his hands.

When toddlers need attention, they will cup a parent's face in their little hands and talk. They need to know parents are listening. Older children, too, need eye contact with parents to feel undivided attention. When someone is looking at you eye-to-eye, you feel that you have that person's attention.

FOCUSED ATTENTION

Focused attention, which is an extension of eye contact, is another component of showing unconditional love. Children know they are important if parents' attention is totally centered on them. Being involved in the things a child does lets them know they are important to a parent: watching their soccer team play and cheering them on, listening as they practice piano, helping with homework, taking a special trip together. A dad told me the other day that he recently drove to a local horse stable and spent two hours one Saturday afternoon just watching his daughter ride her

> *Children know they are important if parents' attention is totally centered on them.*

horse around the riding ring. On the other end of this spectrum, I recently attended a girls high school basketball game where the father of one of the players told me that he and his wife and one other dad were the only parents who "regularly" attended the games! These games are played at night in the high school gym. Do you think the girls whose parents don't attend experience a sufficient amount of attention and unconditional love from their parents?

Focused attention also gives parents the opportunity to discover a child's strengths, weaknesses, and personality characteristics. Parents will learn if their child is good at sports, academics, art, music, or other interests in which they can excel. Parents can also learn how their children communicate with others by watching them play and participate in group activities. Focused attention allows children an opportunity to communicate with a parent and gives parents the chance to affirm children or redirect their behavior. Watching my children interact with others at school and church gave me an opportunity to see specific personality traits and communication skills. I could praise their good qualities and teach them new skills when I saw something undesirable. As a parent, I quickly learned that children don't always *act* the same at home as they act away from home!

JUST DO IT! GETTING INVOLVED WITH CHILDREN

Getting personally involved with children can enhance self-esteem. With little children, parents can play with them, read books to them, and involve them in helping with daily tasks. Teach them to play ball, rake leaves, plant flowers, and other activities that will fascinate children. Grandparents are excellent at involving children in activities and chores and making them feel good about themselves.

Friends become more important and have a more direct influence as children get older.

Encourage other children to come and play so parents can have input in choosing friends and observing their interactions. Friends become more important and have a more direct influence as children get older. Therefore, parents should impact children's choices in friendships at an early age by getting involved in helping choose playmates. Talk to them about characteristics that make good friends. During the teen years, when parental involvement is typically limited in school and extracurricular activities, parents can feel confident in their teens' ability to choose appropriate friends. As much as possible, however, in the adolescent years, stay involved through parent support organizations at school and church leadership positions.

Help build self-esteem by pointing out activities in which children excel. Tell them directly what activities they do well. Actively pursue interests with a child—offer music lessons, play ball (Parents make great coaches!), visit museums, involve children in scouting (How about those weekend camping trips?), pay for dance lessons (But think about those all-day recitals and numerous costumes to purchase!), teach them to swim or ride a bike, and attend children's and youth ministries at church. Praise children for accomplishments. Be sensitive to individual strengths and weaknesses. Don't compare a child to friends and siblings. Encourage self-worth by finding and emphasizing unique strengths and talents in a child. Each child has unique gifts given by God. Psalm 139:13-14 tells us that God "formed my inward parts; [He] covered me in my mother's womb. I will praise [Him], for I am fearfully and wonderfully made."

> *Help build self-esteem by pointing out activities in which children excel.*

Find activities that families can enjoy together, such as camping, vacations, games, bicycling, and water or snow skiing. A favorite story in our family is telling how Roger sledded down a snow-covered mountain slope in France on a plastic tray and wiped out at the bottom! (He still has a scar on his buttocks to remind him of the experience!) When families share activities that are mutually enjoyable, lasting memories are made.

COMPENSATE: FINDING WHAT KIDS DO WELL

Enhance self-esteem in children by discovering what they do well to compensate for shortcomings. Take time to find what strengths children may possess and focus on cultivating them into talents in which they can excel. In working with children and teens, I encounter a variety of strengths and weaknesses: giftedness, learning disabilities, attention-deficit disorders, oppositional defiance, anxiety, depression, and other disorders. As a means to encourage children with identifiable problems, I tell parents to look for anything the child does well and build on that skill. Showing children they have a talent or gift will build self-esteem.

> *Enhance self-esteem in children by discovering what they do well to compensate for shortcomings.*

I worked with a teen who attended a high school for gifted and talented students. He excelled in English but had a learning disability in math. Thankfully, he was planning a journalism career! When children are weak in one area, attention can be focused on their strength in another area. Remember, as parents, we are to "train up a child in the way he should go" (Pr 22:6). Each child has specific strengths that parents can help discover and cultivate.

Children will discover self-esteem when success is achieved. Discuss strengths and weaknesses to help children know themselves better. Talk about developing and focusing on strengths and compensating for weakness. For example, to compensate for weakness in writing skills, emphasize using a computer with a spelling and grammar check to correct writing errors. Children who may be average academically may have talent in art, music, athletics, etc. Focus on and develop individual strengths. Praise success. Pay attention to the positive. De-emphasize the negative.

DISCIPLINE AFFECTS SELF-ESTEEM

How children are disciplined affects self-esteem. Discipline that is too harsh *as well as* too lenient discipline can negatively affect children's self-esteem. For children to respond to discipline and training, they must embrace the values of parents. Children will trust parents and accept discipline when they feel unconditional love. *Unconditional love is critical to appropriate discipline and development of self-esteem.* Parents must always separate the *value* of children from the unacceptable behavior when disciplining a child. Point out the bad behavior. Don't say, "You're a bad boy." Instead, say "You're a good boy and good boys don't do that." When children's emotional needs are fulfilled, they will respond positively to discipline. Without a strong bond of love with parents, children react to parental guidance with anger, hostility, and resentment. Resistance increases as children get older.

> *Unconditional love is critical to appropriate discipline and development of self-esteem.*

How do parents effectively discipline children and build self-esteem? Discipline requires not only pointing out and stopping bad behavior, but teaching new and desired behaviors. For example, if hitting other children out of anger is a problem, parents can say, "When you get angry, you cannot hit your sister. You *can* express anger in another more acceptable way—go to your room and hit your pillow, go outside and ride your bike, come talk to me about your anger. But hitting your sister is unacceptable." Discipline focuses on accepting the emotion (anger, frustration, hatred, etc.) but not the behavior and offers an alternative action.

Here is another example. How can a situation be handled where children are playing ball in the living room too near grandmother's antique lamp? An appropriate response may be, "Throwing the ball inside is not acceptable. Throwing the ball outside is okay. The ball is an outside toy." Again, an alternative behavior is offered to replace the unacceptable behavior. Children need to know the reason for changing behavior. Make them aware that it is in their best interest to do something differently. Children may not always accept a parent's reasoning. A simple explanation is sufficient regardless of whether children agree or not. Don't get caught up in answering the continuous "why?"

> *When children know parents love them, they will trust parents to guide them in the right way.*

It is important to *shape* their *will* without damaging their *spirit*. Much of discipline is teaching appropriate behavior. Harsh punishment with children does not build trust or self-esteem. Appropriate discipline will succeed in changing behavior and nourishing the relationship. When children know parents love them, they will trust parents to guide them in the right way.

Disciplining children appropriately (not too harshly nor too permissively) shows that parents care enough to teach right behaviors. Children need parameters. Security is drawn from knowing where the boundaries are and that parents care enough to enforce them. (See Part III).

CHAPTER 3:

BUILDING SELF-ESTEEM BY WORDS AND LISTENING

TALK! TALK! TALK!

Verbal communication is important to building self-esteem in children. Talk to children the way you talk to friends or coworkers. Do not talk down to them or nag. Show them the same respect you would show your friends. When our children were young, my husband traveled frequently. From sunrise to bedtime, I spent many hours just talking with little people. So I talked to my children as if they were my best friends. My husband's career also afforded my children the opportunity to converse with many college students through their growing-up years. Consequently, both of my children talk freely and easily to people of all ages.

Because verbal communication was important to them as they grew up, they told me lots of things. Some bits of information I wish I didn't know! Moms—whether they want to or not—hear about other moms' boyfriends, fights with husbands, breast implants and stomach reductions, police visits at the neighbor's home, teachers' favorite students, and whose daddy got fired from his job. Try not to react to what you hear. Just shake your head and smile!

Verbal affirmations. To build self-esteem, it is very important that children hear more *positive* words than negative. It is easy to get caught up emphasizing the negative: "Don't do that!"

"Your room is a mess!"

"Why did you spill your milk?"

"You are so disorganized!"

"Can't you ever finish your homework?"

"You made a mess!"

Bite your tongue! What are some things parents can say to *enhance* self-esteem? Think of ways you can encourage rather than criticize. "Let's do this another way!" "Let's finish our homework now and then we can do something special." Point out things children do well. Compliment good attitudes and kind actions:

"You are a happy boy today!"

"You're such a big help to me."

"What would I do without you?"

"I love you."

"You make me laugh."

"You are fun to be with."

"You really like school, . . .art, . . . playing ball, etc."

"You're a good reader."

"I'm so proud of you."

"You're doing a great job."

As they get older, say:

"Your best subject seems to be math, . . . English, . . . science.

"You would do well working on the school newspaper."

"You have good writing skills."

"You would be a good leader in a school club."

"You would be good at playing (a sport, a musical instrument, etc.).

"You're making better decisions lately."

"You have such a great attitude."

"You're a good friend."

"I enjoy the time we spend together."

"I can see you becoming more mature all the time."

Anne Ortlund's book, *Children Are Wet Cement,*[1] has numerous ideas for affirming children. Parents must get in the habit of *affirming* more and *criticizing* less. Much of the world in which we live is negative. We must provide a positive, encouraging home environment in which children can thrive.

"A Picture Is Worth a Thousand Words." Emotional word pictures are tools that Gary Smalley & John Trent talk about using to express feelings both positively and negatively. In *The Language of Love,*[2] they describe how word pictures can be used to communicate thoughts and high value. *An emotional word picture is a communication tool that uses a story or object to activate simultaneously the emotions and intellect of a person.*

> *Parents must get in the habit of affirming more and criticizing less.*

In Genesis 49, Jacob blesses Joseph by saying he is a "fruitful branch [of a tree], a fruitful branch by a spring." Remember the story of Joseph? He was sold into slavery by his brothers, but Pharaoh made him ruler over all of Egypt. During the famine, Joseph's brothers came to him to buy corn in Egypt where it was plentiful (because Joseph had planted it). Joseph literally became a fruitful branch!

Jesus used an emotional word picture to describe Peter. What was it? What did he compare to Peter? Jesus said to Peter, "On this rock I will build My church" (Ma 16:18). Did Peter act like a strong foundation which is characteristic of a rock when he was called as a disciple? Hardly! He flew off the handle, cut off the guard's ear in Gethsemane, and denied Jesus three times before his crucifixion. But

Jesus had this *picture* of Peter, and he *became* the rock foundation that Jesus visualized. After Jesus' resurrection, Peter carried the gospel to the whole world.

Children will become mostly what parents believe they can be and what parents instill in them to achieve. When parents value children as gifts from God (Ps 127:3) and cultivate strengths God has given, children will learn to value themselves.

Let me give you an example of how parents influence self-worth in children. A local newspaper ran a story a few years ago about a star basketball player who played without a hand. She was born without fingers but has excelled not only in basketball but other sports as well. Her father is a high school coach who suggested she participate in sports. Both parents encouraged her and never told her that she had a "disability". The word never became part of her vocabulary. She has excelled in sports and other activities out of sheer determination, raw talent and encouragement from parents who told her "Yes, you can". This young girl became what her parents instilled in her to achieve.

> *Children will become mostly what parents believe they can be and what parents instill in them to achieve.*

What an awesome picture! This is what it is all about—teaching children unconditional love and value! When children feel value and love from parents, they can love others. Children with a high sense of self-esteem will believe they have something positive and productive to contribute. They will be more likely to experience success in family relationships and pass on the blessing to their children. When parents have instilled a healthy self-esteem in children, parenting can be a more rewarding task. By the time children graduate from high school, parents can feel confident their children have the ability to become successful.

LISTEN! (DO YOU HEAR WHAT THEY ARE SAYING?)

Perhaps the most important part of communication is listening, especially as children get older. Learn to talk less and listen more. Parents should set aside more time when they don't have other distractions. Take time when it is quiet—when dinner isn't cooking on the stove, the television is turned off, and younger siblings are in bed. Take time alone with one child to listen to anything he may have to share with you. A child knows he is valuable when a parent spends time with him alone and listens.

If a child is sharing a problem with a parent, use reflective listening to communicate. For example, a child may say, "I hate Jenny!" A parent's first thought is to say "No, you don't. You don't hate anybody. We've taught you better than that!" Bite your tongue, Mom and Dad! *Critical and negative parenting will stifle communication with children.* Be empathetic. Instead, say, "I can see you are upset with Jenny today." Then the child will sense that you understand his feelings. Help a child work through conflict by rewording what he says and allowing him to express frustration *before* advice is offered. He needs to feel he can share his most intimate feelings with you and be accepted.

> *Critical and negative parenting will stifle communication with children.*

A small child needs to express thoughts immediately as thoughts come to mind. Don't put him off when he is trying to talk. Allow him, within reason, to interrupt long enough to say what's on his mind. A small child can't store thoughts and recall them hours later. He will have moved on to something else. Parents may miss a profound or unforgettable question like, "Do worms smile?" or "Mommy, have you ever seen Daddy naked?" To avoid constant interruptions, talk to children in advance about when it is appropriate to interrupt. If parents are on the telephone or entertaining guests, parents can agree on a hand signal to let the parent know a child needs attention. Take fifteen to twenty seconds and let a young child tell what he needs to say. When parents allow short interruptions, a child senses he is valuable.

Getting Kids to Talk. Some kids wake up in the morning talking like a wind-up toy with an Eveready battery. Some burst through the front door after school yelling, "Mom, guess what happened at school today?" Some parents don't have to do anything to get their kids to talk! They just have to take time to listen! Others may require more prodding—sitting down in their room alone, going for a walk or ride in the car, soliciting their help with a project, or spending more time involved in what interests them. Some siblings sense that brothers or sisters may dominate conversations and won't speak up without extra effort from mom or dad.

> *Good communication in the early years is rewarded during the teen years when talking becomes less frequent and sometimes more difficult.*

Create an environment where children can talk to you about anything. Begin at a very early age developing communication skills. Good communication in the early years is rewarded during the teen years when talking becomes less frequent and sometimes more difficult. Encourage children to talk to you about anything. But be ready! Their conversation topics might surprise you!

One afternoon as my kids and I were heading home from school, one child told me a joke he had heard at lunch. I bit my tongue as I listened to the very unsuitable joke and then calmly stated when he was finished, "I'm glad you shared that joke with me first because I do not feel it is appropriate to tell others. Let's just forget that one. I'm glad I had the chance to help you decide what might be okay to tell your friends." Let children know parents can help decide what is an appropriate action or thought.

Children should share their frustrations with parents in a *respectful* manner. Angry outbursts by parents or children interfere with good communication. Writing notes to one another is helpful if extreme emotion is involved in a conflict. Be sure to keep confidences of any information children share. Don't be shocked by what you hear or quick to criticize. Allow plenty of time for a child to talk before drawing a conclusion about the situation. Over-reacting will lead to children's withdrawal of verbal communication. When future opportunities arise to share information, children will recall parents' negative reaction and not confide in them.

Getting Teens to Talk. Adolescence is a stage in which parents may have to discover creative ways to encourage communication. Taking a walk, going shopping, visiting the ice cream shop, or sitting on their bed for a while may encourage conversation. In our family, televisions, VCRs, and computers are all located in living areas of our home to encourage children to spend more time in the family rooms as opposed to alone in their bedrooms. Making family rooms more enticing provides opportunities to interact.

> *Adolescence is a stage in which parents may have to discover creative ways to encourage communication.*

Franklin Graham, son of evangelist Billy Graham, said he always had access to his dad.[3] Franklin said he could walk into his dad's office during a staff meeting and his dad would stop and take time to listen to Franklin. Children need to know they are important to parents and are worthy of their time.

BLESSING CHILDREN COMMUNICATES VALUE

In *The Blessing,*[4] Gary Smalley & John Trent write about children's need for parental approval and the importance of self-esteem based on biblical principles of the family blessing.

In the Old Testament, Abraham's family received the blessing God had promised (Ge 12:1-3), and God's blessing was passed from generation to generation, right up to the birth of Christ. The Old Testament blessing is no longer needed because Christ's sacrifice on the cross for the sins of the whole world made God's blessing available to all people.

> *The blessing communicated unconditional love and acceptance to children.*

Blessings in the Old Testament were not just spiritual blessings. Family blessings within a Jewish family were also passed on to future generations. The story of Esau and Jacob (Ge 27) tells of a brother (Esau) whose father's blessing as the firstborn was stolen by the trickery of his younger brother (Jacob). Esau grieved because he was stripped of his rightful blessing. In biblical times, *the blessing communicated unconditional love and acceptance to children.* Blessings today can still communicate these values to children.

Blessing Children with Prayer and Scripture. Prayer can be used to communicate blessing. Spend time praying specifically for each child. Pray while washing their clothes, packing lunches, driving in the car (don't close your eyes!), or after tucking them in bed at night. Pray *with* your children. Children need to hear their parents pray positive things for them and thank God for specific gifts and talents in each child.

Use Scripture to give a blessing. "Lord, may (child's name) trust you with all his heart, and may he lean not on his own understanding. But may he seek to know what you would want him to do always. You have promised to make his path straight (Pr 3:5-6). Lord, may (child's name) obey his parents in all things because this pleases you (Col 3:20)." This should be a parent's personal favorite! Find an appropriate verse and insert a child's name!

SUMMARY

Self-esteem is essential to the healthy and successful development of children. Self-esteem should come from a home environment that communicates unconditional love and value to children. Demonstration of love by physical touch, eye contact and focused attention, positive verbal communication, affirmations, involvement with kids, effective discipline, compensation for weakness and reinforcement of strengths, communication of love through blessings, and emotional word pictures are all effective ways to build self-esteem.

PART II

COMMUNICATION FOR A LIFELONG RELATIONSHIP

CHAPTER 4:

POSITIVE COMMUNICATION

Darrell Scott, in *Rachel's Tears*[1], tells a story of a beautiful conversation with his daughter, Rachel:

> Rachel had been out late one night and was cited for breaking the Littleton curfew . . . so I had to take her downtown to pay a fine. She hadn't done anything wrong, but the city is strict about its curfew, and she had violated it. Afterward, we were sitting at my dining room table. We didn't purposely sit down to have a heart-to-heart talk. We just started talking, and suddenly I found myself saying things that surprised me. I realized that I was in the middle of a father-daughter conversation with someone who once was a little girl but had gradually become a big girl. Graduation was still a year away for Rachel, but I began sharing with her about all kinds of things.
>
> "I talked about how I hadn't always been a perfect dad. I told her that I tried to do the best I could, but that I was sorry we hadn't spent as much time together as I had wanted to. . . . As we talked, I told her that I loved her unconditionally. . . .

Rachel had a unique way of tilting her head to the side when she was thinking seriously, and she was doing that during this talk. And I remember her beautiful smile. Our conversation was intense. By the time we finished we were both crying. She got up and came around toward where I was sitting at the table, and I got up and met her at the head of the table. We hugged and sobbed together.

What a beautiful story about how to communicate unconditional love to children! *Raising children is a lifelong commitment!* That may not be something you wanted to hear! However, relationships with children do change through the years! Toddlers will let go of mom's legs and venture out on their own. Six-year-olds with backpacks and lunch boxes in hand take that first step

> *When parents are successful in raising children, positive relationships will blossom.*

into the classroom for a full day of school (Being childless from 8 a.m. to 3 p.m. seems like an eternity for moms new to the school experience. You'll get adjusted to the schedule very soon). Middle-schoolers will beg to meet friends at the skating rink on Friday night (beware!). Teens will grab the car keys and drive off never to be seen again (except when they are hungry or need sleep).

When parents are successful in raising children, positive relationships will blossom. As children become mature young adults, parents become friends and confidants. Families actually *enjoy* doing fun things together—without arguing! Developing healthy and effective communication *now* with children will increase the chances of a positive relationship in the future.

COMMUNICATE RESPECT AND LOVE

How we relate to children while we are raising them is important. Parents desire to develop a relationship of trust, unconditional love and value, and mutual respect with children. To achieve this, parents must decide *how* to effectively shape a positive relationship with children.

Not long ago, I sat down with an older retired couple whom I have known for a number of years. (I went to high school with their children.) They talked about each of their children and how much they enjoyed them and their families. This cou-

> *The right method of communication is required to foster long-term relationships.*

ple's world still revolves around their family even though the children are grown and have children of their own. The relationships are positive and rewarding. They spend time together at family dinners, baseball games, dance recitals, and sleepovers with the grandchildren. That seems rare today! But a loving, nurturing lifelong relationship is attainable with children when the parent-child relationship is nurtured through the growing-up years.

The right method of communication is required to foster long-term relationships. With some children it is easy to nag, remind, criticize, cajole, threaten, lecture, question, advise, evaluate, probe, and ridicule. How much of communication consists of these negative tactics? Although usually done with good intentions these methods diminish, rather than improve, communication with children. Imagine lecturing or criticizing your friends? How would they react? They probably wouldn't want to be friends or would even avoid contact with a person who is constantly critical. Parents should treat children with the same respect and dignity that is afforded to friends and coworkers.

When dealing with children, treat them the way you want to be treated. Children have the same needs as adults: affirmation, acceptance, love, positive communication, and compassion.

Think about what adults need when they are upset. Do they need time alone? Maybe children do, too. Do parents need someone who will listen, understand and empathize? Children have the same feelings and needs. How parents respond to children determines the kind of relationship that will develop in the future. If parents are empathetic, understanding, and attentive when children are upset, children will learn to trust parents and will desire to communicate with them.

CHAPTER 5:

YAKETY-YAK: HOW WE TALK TO KIDS

Most communication deals with *words*. It's interesting that God made only humans to use words, although sometimes I think my dog can talk. I know I can decipher her whine and the look in her eyes even without the words. Maybe I should be glad that she can't talk! She might tell all my secrets but still love me anyway!

Words have power for both good and evil. Hitler's evil words taught propaganda and hatred. His words led to a world war and the killing of millions of innocent people. Never underestimate the potential power of evil words and thoughts. Our nation has recently experienced the consequences of the power of negative words and thoughts through terrorist attacks on our cities (September 11, 2001) and the resulting war against these terrorists abroad. Words can also have power in a positive way. Jesus used words for good. He taught love and forgiveness with words—words that are still read, studied, and followed today. Every word spoken affects children for good or evil. Words can kill their inner spirit. Parents can harm or

> *Every word spoken affects children for good or evil.*
>
> *What comes out of our mouths is reflection of what is in our hearts.*

build children's self-esteem through words, and these words speak volumes about unconditional love. Positive communication should be much more prevalent than negative words and actions. *What comes out of our mouths is reflection of what is in our hearts.*

WATCH YOUR WORDS!

A young mother shared her story with me about difficulty with a thirteen-year-old son who was constantly lying, engaging in fights at school, and failing classes. The mother was so exasperated with the child's behavior (understandably) that she was constantly nagging and criticizing him. She had even threatened to send him to another state to live with his dad. Among the many ideas we discussed about the young man, I shared with her the idea of discovering situations in which positive reinforcement and affirmation could be given. For example, giving positive attention when he *does* clean up his room, bring home a good conduct grade at school, or spend time doing homework. Constant negative words and actions from both sides snowball into a bad situation. (We also worked up a contract of behavior and consequences so that there was no need for nagging or discussion about unacceptable behavior).

Words can be used to destroy or control. Verbal abuse, ridicule, cursing, and lying are all evil ways to use words. H. Norman Wright, in his book *The Power of a Parent's Words*,[1] talks about how words are toxic weapons that parents use to hurt children. They contaminate and wound, poison and destroy children emotionally. Launched like combat missiles, critical words are used to attack a child's behavior, appearance, intelligence, competence, or value as a person. It is easy to get caught up in negative verbal attacks. Parenthood can be frustrating! Children will *act* like children: they will spill things, cry at inappropriate times, fight with their siblings, kick the cat, say things they shouldn't, fall off bicycles, get sick at the most inopportune times, misbehave in the grocery store, talk in church, make bad grades, or play with expensive tools! Remember that children can't be expected to *act* like adults. (Even though some adults continue to act like children, the opposite is not usually true!)

That reminds me of a story of childish behavior—from an adult. An acquaintance recently visited my church for Wednesday night dinner and Bible study. He sat at a table with a friend, only to be reprimanded by a long-time church member who accused him of sitting in her seat! This man was gracious, got up, took his plate, and sat at another table! (*Lord, help adults to act like adults*. . . . What is that terminology about a "second childhood"?)

WORDS MAKE AN IMPRESSION

Be patient in training children and nurturing them into adulthood. They *will* grow up, but until that happens, consider their little hearts and minds like wet cement—very impressionable to what parents say and do! Children will become what parents instill in them to become. Think about dance teachers who raise dancers. Musicians who raise children who love music. Preachers whose children grow up to be ministers or missionaries. Teachers who produce teachers. Confident business leaders who raise children who are self-assertive in their own business. Children will not always follow in the career paths of parents, but these patterns are evidence of the impact parents make on children.

Compare those parents to parents who are verbally abusive to children, constantly criticize, and only show love conditionally. These children will likely grow up without confidence to succeed and with a negative view of the world.

Many parents are guilty of "binge" criticism with children. Situations occur in which parents verbally "beat up" on a particular child for every infraction or attitude.

Rebellious behavior or underachievement in a child, job stresses, health concerns, marriage difficulties, and other problems can result in negative communication. Recognize "binge" criticism and deal with it. Replace negative talk with effective communication—words that build up and encourage instead of tearing down.

Be willing to say "I'm sorry" when a wrong has been committed against children. They can be the most forgiving people on earth. They need to see that parents make mistakes and are willing to ask forgiveness. Children will learn to trust when they witness parents' honesty and vulnerability to error.

A mother whose teenager stayed in trouble with parents, school, and even the juvenile authorities during the high school years recently shared that she had begun to realize mistakes made in raising the child. Support groups and counseling have helped her deal with this wayward teen but also have targeted some parenting mistakes. She discussed on several occasions how she was overly critical of her teenager, not encouraging him in his pursuits. She admitted to not being in touch with his friends, not knowing where he was or what he was doing on the weekends. She recently wrote a letter to the teen, who is now in college, to apologize for mistakes she made as a mother. The teen has also recognized his own rebellion and drug abuse and is remorseful for the pain caused to his family. Emotional healing is beginning to take place as the two recognize shortcomings and admit mistakes.

> *Be willing to say "I'm sorry" when a wrong has been committed against children.*

CHAPTER 6:

STOP FIGHTING!

What we say and *how* we speak is important to good communication and to helping resolve conflict with children. Shouting and name-calling should not be part of communication. There are many aspects to effectively resolving conflict: empathizing with their feelings, reflective listening, giving advice, and talking through consequences and behavior.

EMPATHY AND ADVICE

Helping children deal with conflict first involves empathizing with the child's feelings. To develop credibility with children, parents must connect by understanding their feelings. When a child comes to a parent with a conflict that needs to be resolved, talk through the problem so that each side's point of view is discussed and understood. Consider alternatives to solutions by offering advice on how to deal with conflict. Parents' advice is sometimes accepted without question. You may say, "Consider this" or "I think you should . . ." Children may take the advice without hesitation. Sharing a personal experience of conflict may increase credibility in solving problems. (Don't keep

> *What we say and how we speak is important to good communication and to helping resolve conflict with children.*

telling them the same story over and over for years! They will say, "I know. I know. Mom, you've told me that story before!") The child may realize that you can identify with his problem. Share new stories and fresh ideas you learn along the way. Keep talking about lessons you learn in dealing with others.

The downside to only offering advice is that it does not always help children solve their own problems. Only offering advice may lead to dependence on parents, and children won't learn to think through resolutions to problems. Also, when offering advice for solving a problem, parents may be blamed if a solution does not work. Strong-willed children tend to resist taking advice.

Use reflective listening to understand and clarify the child's feelings. When they share frustrations with you, empathize with their feelings. When "Sweet Sam" encounters "Billy the Bully" at school, parents may say, "You're angry that Billy is picking on you. It seems to me that you feel Billy doesn't like you and wants to hurt and embarrass you." Let them feel empathy without making judgments about their feelings. The child may say, "Yes, that is exactly how I feel!" He will be more likely to trust the parent to help him work through this situation because he knows the parent understands his feeling. Allowing children to talk through situations while reinforcing an understanding of their feelings gives children the opportunity to verbalize frustrations and work out possible solutions. Children may be more open to accepting parents' solutions when they feel parents understand their emotions.

BRAINSTORMING

Brainstorming is another method of exploring alternatives by engaging kids in offering alternatives and considering consequences. Help kids to find solutions to problems by offering ideas and questions. Exploring alternatives may be a more effective way to help strong-willed children with resolving conflict. (Parents with a strong-willed child recognize this trait as soon as the child can speak! "No" and "I can do it myself" become part of this child's vocabulary very early.) Teach important critical thinking skills by brainstorming alternatives with children. This empowers them to solve problems on their own. Ask them how they should handle the situation. Listen to what they say. Discuss possible consequences for them to consider.

For example, if a child is having difficulty with the "bully" at school. Ask what he thinks he should do. He might say, "hit him back", "tell him to leave me alone", or "tell the teacher". A parent may ask, "Shall we look at some things you could do about this?" "If you're interested in getting along with Billy, what are some things you could do?" "If Billy tries to pick a fight with you, what are your options?" Suggest talking to the bully and trying to be friends or avoiding situations where he would be around the bully. Talk to the child about consequences and outcomes of each choice so they can make the right decision about handling the conflict. Extract as many ideas from children as possible. Help *them* think of solutions. This stimulates reasoning processes and gives them confidence to determine solutions.

> *Teach important critical thinking skills by brainstorming alternatives with children.*

Then, assist in choosing a solution. "Which idea do you think is the best one?" "Do you think it is best to hit him back? Tell the teacher? Walk away? Talk to him?" Help children to evaluate the various possibilities. This places responsibility of the decision on them and encourages confidence in their ability to solve problems.

Discuss the probable results of the decision. "What do you think will happen if you do that?" "Will he respond to you trying to make friends?" "Will you get in trouble by hitting Billy back?" "Will the teacher deal with the situation if you talk to her about it?" Look at possible consequences *before* making a decision.

Obtain a commitment. Ask, "What have you decided to do?" "When are you going to do this?" This gets them to make the decision and stick to it. If possible don't allow procrastination. After a decision is made, plan a time for evaluation. "How long will you try this?" "When shall we discuss this again?" When a wrong decision by the child is obvious, share your disagreement with children and give reasons for choosing another solution.

Direct intervention by parents may be required to prevent a crucial mistake with long-term consequences. For instance, if Sam hits Billy at school, he may get suspended! If possible, however, allow them to make the wrong decision and learn from natural consequences of behavior. The experience increases your credibility as a worthy source of advice. (Don't say "I told you so"!)

Guide children through these steps to good decision making. Learning to explore alternatives will help children become critical thinkers and make choices on their own. Thinking skills are an important tool that parents can develop in children to become confident, successful, and independent adults.

TWELVE TIPS FOR COMMUNICATING EFFECTIVELY

Teaching an eleventh grade Sunday school class, I usually present a lesson on communicating with parents. I came up with "Twelve Tips for Talking with Parents without Ticking Them Off." These tips can be helpful to parents, as well:

1. Treat each other the way you want to be treated. Consider how you speak to others and ask if you

would want others to communicate with you in the same way. Talk to children in a soft tone of voice. Speak warmly, lovingly, and humbly (Ma 7:12; Pr 21:23).

2. Be honest and open with children. Express concerns about friends, schoolwork, feelings, goals—this builds trust with them. Share personal experiences (Pr 4:24; 12:22).

3. Talk about issues with them: underage drinking, sex, illegal drugs, inappropriate movies/television shows, bad language, a friend's behavior. Listening to their point of view helps you learn their values. Remind them where you stand. Again, appropriate communication builds trust (Ga 5:19—6:2).

4. Ask advice. Take advice. Don't be afraid to ask your children's advice on issues (Pr 1:8-9; 4:23).

5. Show respect and honor to others. Respect and honor should be mutual between parents and children. Parents teach honor and respect by first demonstrating it to their children and others (Ep 6:1-3).

6. Show appreciation for all they do for you. Say "thank you" often—and mean it! Parents and children are more willing to give when each feels appreciated (1 Th 5:16-18).

7. Choose the right time and place to discuss issues. Give advance notice when you need to talk. Parents need a chance to set aside responsibilities and focus on the child. This advice works for kids, too. Be sensitive to

your child's mood before tackling a sensitive issue (Pr 15:23).

8. Communicate in positive ways. Don't always be negative or nag. Learn to be more affirming with each other and carefully word criticisms (Pr 15:28; Ma 7:1-2).

9. Control your anger. Do not raise your voice or say something disrespectful. This damages credibility and the likelihood that an issue can be solved without bitter feelings (Pr 15:1; Jam 3:6-10).

10. Use "I" words when communicating your feelings: "I *feel* like you tried to hurt me when . . ." Pointing a finger by saying, "You hurt me..." only builds a defense against your case (Pr 15:2).

11. Be accountable for behavior. Accept responsibility for wrong decisions or behavior. Say "I am sorry" when you have disappointed them. When both parents and children adhere to this rule, trust is built (Ep 4:31-32).

12. Listen. Try to see their point of view. Sometimes we react to what we *think* someone is saying or feeling without fully knowing their point of view. Listening to their side without interrupting them is critical to knowing their point of view (Pr 1:8).

COMMUNICATING 'I' INSTEAD OF POINTING THE 'YOU' FINGER

Tip number ten suggests using "I" messages instead of pointing the "You" finger. Verbal attacks on children will lead them to tune out and not listen. ("Talk to the hand because I'm not listening," as kids say today.) When parents do all the talking and no listening, children will withdraw and will not talk because they don't expect parents to hear what they are saying. *Try not to interrupt them!* To influence behavior, parents and children must be able to communicate in a manner in which feelings, thoughts, and intentions are understood by each other.

Conflict in communication is sometimes caused by "you" messages. The "you" message lays blame and conveys criticism to children. It is a verbal attack that suggests children are at fault. "You did not take out the trash today. You are so irresponsible and lazy." What message does the child hear? "I am irresponsible and lazy". The parent wants to convey the message that he is not pleased because the trash was not taken out. But the attack was on the child *not* the specific behavior.

"I" messages simply describe how children's behavior makes you feel.

Appropriately used, "I" messages keep communication open, which aids in problem-solving.

In contrast, "I" messages simply describe how children's behavior makes you feel. The message focuses on the person speaking, not the other person. An "I" message reports what the person feels and doesn't assign blame to someone else. "When you don't take out the trash after I ask you to, the kitchen has a bad odor. I feel frustrated because I feel like I have to do all the work." This response gives the message that you are unhappy about the trash not being disposed of rather than being dissatisfied with the character of the child.

"I" messages are expressed in a way that is not threatening to the other person and does not cause defensiveness. Therefore, it is a more desirable method of communicating and will be more likely to elicit a favorable outcome to conflict. Don't use a harsh tone of voice or a judgmental attitude when expressing "I" messages. State your feelings calmly.

When anger is allowed into the conversation, communication is stifled. Appropriately used, "I" messages keep communication open, which aids in problem-solving.

How to Use an "I" Message. "I" messages tell children how their behavior interferes with parents and how parents feel about this interference. It allows expression of feelings without assigning blame. Children will learn to respect others' feelings and behave in a way that is pleasing.

When parents are entertaining guests, children seem to want more attention. They interrupt parents and guests with questions and demands. Instead of saying, "You are interrupting us. Don't bother me now," say, "When there are interruptions, we cannot talk with each other." This is an "I" message that communicates displeasure without a personal attack.

> *Good communication with children begins with a foundation of mutual respect.*

"I" messages can be used in other situations to change behavior without placing blame. When children leave toys scattered all over the floor, try saying "When toys are left on the floor, I am afraid someone will fall over them and get hurt." This lets children know behavior needs to be changed without placing personal blame. "I" messages can be used when a child won't go to sleep on time, when they fight with a sibling, or when homework is not done. ("I want you to get plenty of sleep so you will be rested for school." "It hurts me to see the children I love fighting with each other." "I know you are a responsible student and responsible students do their homework.") Almost any situation with children can be handled with an "I" message.

The purpose of "I" messages is to keep communication open with children and to achieve a positive, effective solution to problems that doesn't lower self-esteem. Remember, children are like wet cement!

Good communication with children begins with a foundation of mutual respect. This is not to say that parents should give up authority. Parents must maintain the authority role. It can be achieved by methods that foster respect and communication. Choose to listen carefully and include children's ideas when dealing with conflict and communicate in a respectful way to encourage positive relationships rather than negative ones.

BEWARE OF USING ANGER

It's sometimes normal for parents to be angry with children. Anger is okay when channeled correctly. Ephesians 4:26 says, "Be angry and do not sin." The problem is not in the anger itself but in the purpose of the anger: Do parents speak angry words to get control of a situation,

When children's undesirable behavior provokes parents to anger, children actually gain power or revenge because the parents' reaction through angry words shows children that they can control another's emotions.

seek revenge on children, or insure winning an argument? When children's undesirable behavior provokes parents to anger, children actually gain power or revenge because the parents' reaction through angry words shows children that they can control another's emotions. This can become a power play with children. Not falling into this power play trap with kids is important not only in communication but also in appropriate discipline (which will be discussed in Part III).

CHAPTER 7:

SPEAK ANOTHER LANGUAGE

WORD PICTURES

Communicating effectively can be enhanced by the use of emotional word pictures which allows children to feel what the parent feels. John Trent & Gary Smalley explain the concept of emotional word pictures in *The Language of Love*.[1] In Part I, I talked about how emotional word pictures can enhance self-esteem. In this chapter, the focus is on enhancing the ability to communicate thoughts and emotions by using an emotional word picture.

> *Communicating effectively can be enhanced by the use of emotional word pictures which allows children to feel what the parent feels.*

What Is an Emotional Word Picture? Word pictures capture an emotional feeling apart from the literal meaning of words (See chapter 3).

Stimulating emotions and intellect together causes the person to *experience* words, not just hear them. This type of communication brings to life the thoughts being expressed. It helps to clarify ideas and feelings.

It is important to use word pictures in which children can easily identify. For example, if a child plays soccer, a word picture that relates to soccer can be given because the child is familiar with the sport. If a child has been disobedient, a parent may say, "Honey, you know how you feel when a player from an opposing team comes up behind you when you are running with the ball and slide tackles you from behind? Even though you know the referee will give him a yellow card penalty for that behavior, you still feel cheated out of maybe scoring a goal and could possibly be physically injured because of the player's behavior. That is the way I feel when you disobey me. I feel cheated and betrayed because you do not do what I asked."

> *A child can identify with the feelings and thoughts when explained by a word picture because they can experience the feeling personally.*

A child can identify with the feelings and thoughts when explained by a word picture because they can *experience* the feeling personally. They understand how a parent feels because they relate their own feelings from the word picture presented. A child may say to himself, "I understand how Mom feels when I disobey her because I know how I feel when a player slide tackles me." This emotional word picture also communicates an "I" message.

How Do Word Pictures Work? Word pictures work because they grab and direct attention to the problem. Advertisers use word pictures effectively. Can you recognize these advertising logos?

1. "You're in Good Hands"
2. "Own a Piece of the Rock"
3. "Like a Good Neighbor"

(Answers: 1. Allstate 2. Prudential 3. State Farm).

Word pictures bring communication to life. One can feel the emotion. It produces a physical effect. Think about how suspense novels produce emotion in the reader! Words arouse emotion when one can picture the situation.

Word pictures help children to store important thoughts in memory because they can *feel* the situation. "When I get slide tackled in a soccer game, it really hurts and makes me angry. When I disobey Mom, she feels hurt and angry, too." Word pictures trigger an emotion that both people can feel. It produces a connection in conflicting situations.

A Biblical Example of a Word Picture. Scripture is filled with emotional word pictures. Here is a familiar example: Do you remember the story of David and Bathsheba? A quick synopsis: David saw Bathsheba bathing on her rooftop one evening and thought she was beautiful. He had her brought to him even though she was married to Uriah, the Hittite. He slept with her and she became pregnant. So David sent for her husband who was in battle. David tried to

> *Word pictures trigger an emotion that both people can feel.*

force Uriah to go home and sleep with Bathsheba, so he would think the baby was his. (Sound like a modern day soap opera?) When Uriah refused because he was a dedicated soldier at war, David called him in to eat and drink with him. David got him drunk, but still Uriah would not go home to Bathsheba out of respect for his fellow soldiers. So David sent Uriah to the front lines of war where David had him killed in battle so that he could marry Bathsheba.

As you can imagine, David's actions did not please God. So God had Nathan, David's court adviser, confront David about his sin. Nathan used an emotional word picture (2 Sa 12:1-7) to expose David's sin. Nathan told David a story about a poor man whose only lamb was slaughtered to feed a rich man. David was enraged at the rich man who took the lamb. He told Nathan that the rich man should be killed and the lamb restored fourfold. Nathan then said to David, "You are the man!" (2 Sa 12:7). Through the story Nathan told of the poor man's lamb, David was able to recognize his sin against Uriah, Bathsheba, and most of all, God.

> *A child will typically express his love language to others in the same way the child wants to receive love.*

An emotional word picture is a powerful method of communication because it allows the expression of feelings effectively with a word picture that the listener can identify with but doesn't feel accused by. Word pictures help us avoid bitterness and anger.

LOVE LANGUAGES

Besides influencing self-esteem, knowing a child's love language can also affect communication with children. *The Five Love Languages of Children* by Gary Chapman and Ross Campbell identify physical touch, quality time, acts of service, words of affirmation, and receiving gifts as love languages that communicate unconditional love.[2] Children will respond to one or more of these love languages which can be used to communicate feelings and thoughts. Parents can truly love children but not effectively communicate love with them if they don't respond based on specific love languages.

How Are Love Languages Identified? How do parents know a child's love language? Observe children. Look at the ways a child shows love to others. *A child will typically express his love language to others in the same way the child wants to receive love.* John is six years old. When dad comes home from work, John jumps in his lap, rubs dad's head, and throws his arms around dad. What is John saying? He wants to be touched and held. John's love language is physical touch. John will respond to his parents' love when they physically touch and hold him.

Michelle is also six years old. She lives next door to John. When Michelle's dad comes home, he faces a different scenario. Michelle says excitedly, "Come here, Dad. I want to show you something. Come with me." Dad says, "Wait a minute. Let me read the paper." Michelle leaves dad alone but returns in fifteen minutes to ask dad again, "Dad, come to my room. I want to show you something." Again, dad makes an excuse. Michelle leaves and comes back again. "Please Dad, come with me." What does Michelle need? She needs dad to spend time with her. Her love language is quality time.

If a child is frequently making special gifts for loved ones, wrapping them up and joyfully presenting them, what do you think his love language is? Receiving gifts. This child needs to frequently receive gifts and favors to feel love.

Amanda is a child who always wants to be the helper. She wants to take care of a little brother or sister and help mommy and daddy with chores. Her love language is exhibited through acts of service. She needs loved ones to do things for her and with her so that she feels loved.

If a child is often complimenting others, his love language is probably words of affirmation. He needs to hear "I love you," "You're such special boy," "You're a good helper," "Mommy is so proud of you."

If children's love languages are not met, they will not feel love they need to grow and develop into well-adjusted adults. Love must be communicated in the way children can receive it, i.e., love language. When children don't feel love, they will look for love and affection outside the family circle and many times in undesirable ways.

In the teen years, if teenagers do not feel love from their family, they will search for it through peer groups and sexual intimacy. This is a special concern in single parent homes where children do not receive the consistent daily contact with the non-custodial parent.

> *Communicating effectively with children requires learning new ways to communicate ideas and feelings.*

Communicating effectively with children requires learning new ways to communicate ideas and feelings. Emotional word pictures elicit feelings that can be shared between two people and help to resolve conflict. Learning how a child receives love (or which love language is predominant) helps a parent to communicate more effectively.

CHAPTER 8:

ARE YOU LISTENING?

A very important part of communication to consider is *listening*. Listening allows one to hear and understand another's point of view. Parents can know children by attentively listening to them. One dad told me that he loves going on trips with his son because when the two of them get together alone, the son talks constantly. "I learn so much about him and his inner, deep thoughts when we are alone," he said, "just the two of us without any interruptions. He has so many things to say that he doesn't share when other siblings are demanding my time." Take the time to be a good listener with children.

GOOD LISTENING SKILLS

Aspects of good listening skills include the following:

> Maintain good eye contact. Listening requires focused attention by looking into the eyes of the person who is talking (not watching TV, reading the paper, or cooking dinner).

> Reinforce children's conversations by nodding and paraphrasing what is said (reflective listening). One child told me about hitting a softball that accidentally struck a teammate in the head. I replied to him by saying, "You really feel bad about what happened. . . ." The reply reassured the child that I was listening and could empathize with the story.

GOOD LISTENING SKILLS (continued)

Clarify what the child is saying by restating what the child said and asking, "Is this what you mean?"
Actively move away from distractions that might interrupt good communication. Find a quiet place to talk without television noise or siblings talking.
Be committed to understanding what was said, even when angry or upset about a situation. "I need to understand what you are thinking . . . feeling . . . the reason for your actions. . . ."
Listen with empathy. Try to understand a child's behavior from *his* point of view.
Listen with awareness. Compare what is being said to what is known about the situation. Decide whether what the child says is contradicting or makes sense with what you know about the situation. Check nonverbal cues: tone of voice, facial expression, arms folded. "Your frown seems to say that you disagree." "Your tone of voice tells me that you are angry."

Children don't always know how to effectively communicate their feelings or understand their emotions. They may act out as a response to problems. In talking to a family whose child was in trouble at school, I learned that the child had been suspended several times for fighting. Mom was frustrated. The stepfather did not know what to do either. In talking with the child and parents, we discovered the behavior was a result of the child's frustration with not having regular contact with his biological father. The mom and stepfather were on his case because of school problems and were not aware of the child's real anxiety in dealing with his father.

Their focus was on his behavior, but they had not spent time talking with him to discover that the behavior was only a reaction to his real problem. Effectively communicating with a child can reveal the reason for undesirable behavior.

RESULTS OF GOOD COMMUNICATION

Adults know how important it is to have someone who will listen. Finding a friend or loved one who is empathetic and attentive encourages children to want to spend time with that person and seek their advice. Effective listening will encourage children to communicate with parents.

Effective communication can produce a lifelong positive relationship. Children will continue to want a relationship with parents. My mom is one of my best friends. She listens, understands, gives advice, and encourages—especially when I am writing!

Remember the story I shared with you at the beginning of this section about Darrell Scott and his daughter, Rachel? The conversation between Rachel and her dad was their last conversation together. Rachel was one of the thirteen people gunned down by

> *Effective listening will encourage children to communicate with parents.*

two fellow students at Columbine High School in Littleton, Colorado. Darrell Scott's response concerning his last conversation with his daughter was this:

> I didn't know at the time that it was to be our good-bye talk, but looking back on it now, I know there was nothing left unsaid between us. It was a total openness, and I believe that God ordained that talk. . . . I would never have expected that Rachel would be taken from me only a few days later, but I thank God that we had such a heartfelt talk together.[1]

Darrell Scott clings to the memory of his last meaningful conversation with his daughter. I wonder how we would talk to our kids if we *knew* it might be our last conversation. Resolve to make every conversation meaningful and positive.

SUMMARY

Effective communication with children will produce lifelong relationships that will be cherished within the family. To nurture that relationship, show children genuine interest in their thoughts and feelings and be willing to work through conflict. Many techniques for effective communication help parents to be successful: using positive words, "I" messages and emotional word pictures; exploring alternatives; knowing children's love language; and most important: listening.

PART III

EFFECTIVE DISCIPLINE AND TRAINING

CHAPTER 9:

MAKING KIDS MIND IS GOOD FOR KIDS, TOO!

Charles Swindoll tells the following story through a message on cassette titled "Shaping the Will with Wisdom."[1] He tells of a fourteen-year-old girl who wrote these words:

> My problem is one you probably don't hear much. My daddy is a doctor and he is very busy. My mom is a champion golfer and she is at the club most afternoons when I come home from school. On weekends, they party, and sometimes I worry about it because they drink too much, especially lately. But what really bothers me is how they let me do almost anything I want to. They never tell me when to come in. And I can go anywhere. You might think, *How lucky she is!* I tell you, that is not how I feel about it. What bothers me is that I wonder if I am all that ready to decide everything by myself?

These are words from a lonely and insecure fourteen-year-old girl who desperately needs boundaries. Children need to know the rules by which to live. Consistent and fair rules provide security. The question she asked in the last sentence assures us that guidelines are needed.

Is discipline necessary in raising children? Absolutely! Whose responsibility is it to discipline children? . . . . *Parents!* Sometimes I would like to discipline other peoples' children! Like the two-year-old in the doctor's waiting room recently who continued to emit this shrill scream at the top of his lungs and hit his mother in frustration because she would not meet his constant demands! But that is not my right to discipline *her* child. If this book had been completed, I would have handed her a copy!

> *The goal of discipline is to teach children appropriate and desirable behavior.*

WHAT IS DISCIPLINE?

What is discipline? The word "discipline" comes from the Latin word that means "to teach." The goal of discipline is to teach children *appropriate* and *desirable* behavior. Teaching appropriate behavior is the positive side of discipline. When children do not behave in a manner instructed by parents, negative discipline is necessary. This is called punishment or correction.

TWO SIDES OF DISCIPLINE

Discipline has two sides: instruction and correction. One positive. The other negative. Teaching a desired behavior should extinguish an undesired behavior. For example, teach a five-year-old to place dirty clothes in a clothes hamper by being there when he undresses and walking with him to the hamper. Instruct him to put dirty clothes in the hamper each time he undresses so his clothes will be washed and won't be left on the floor. Praise him verbally when his clothes hit the hamper! After a while (some learn sooner than others), the behavior will be learned and clothes will automatically go in the hamper... most of the time (without instruction and reinforcement).

When teaching doesn't produce pleasing results, correction may be needed. Using the dirty clothes example, if occasionally dirty clothes are found on the floor, parents may remind the child where dirty clothes belong. If this is a frequent behavior, correction may be needed. Say, "I found dirty clothes on your floor today. You will have to wash them yourself. Each day dirty clothes are found on the floor, you will be responsible for laundry." Younger children will require some supervision and assistance. They will most likely learn it is less work to put clothes in the laundry basket than to wash clothes themselves!

Teaching Is Positive Discipline. Instruction is the preferred method of discipline. In the Old Testament, discipline was closely associated with training, instruction, and knowledge on the one side, and correction, reproof, and punishment on the other side. In Deuteronomy 6:6-9 we read, "And these words which I command you today shall be in your heart; you shall teach them diligently to your children, and shall talk of them when you sit in your house, when you walk by the way, when you lie down, and when you rise up. You shall bind them as a sign on your hand, and they shall be as frontlets between your eyes. You shall write them on the doorposts of your house and on your gates."

> *Teaching children appropriate behavior is ongoing. Even when parents aren't consciously giving instructions, children are learning by observing their behavior.*

Teaching children appropriate behavior is ongoing. Even when parents aren't consciously giving instructions, children are learning by observing their behavior. Especially when children are young, many behaviors and attitudes *must* be taught. Children aren't born into the world knowing how to behave. Behavior is learned (mostly from parents). Parents are responsible for instructing children how to live.

It is a true joy as children grow to watch them behave in pleasing and responsible ways. As a parent of college students, it is a reward to witness young adults who are independent and responsible. Teaching produces positive results.

When Positive Teaching Doesn't Work. Positive instruction doesn't always work. When children disobey, negative discipline is warranted. Some parents only discipline by punishment rather than positive teaching. Because punishment is negative, it should be used sparingly and only when instruction doesn't work. Punishment takes on many forms: privileges taken away, time-out, over-correction, and spanking. Taking away privileges is usually more effective with older children and teens. For example, when a teenager comes home Saturday night after curfew, the privilege of going out the next Saturday night can be taken away or an earlier curfew given.

Over-correction can be used effectively with children preschool age and older. An example of over-correction is when a child continues to track mud on the kitchen floor (*AFTER* being told to take off muddy shoes outside). He can be required to mop the entire kitchen floor (not just the muddy part). This is over-correction. *When the punishment requires more effort than the original task, the task itself becomes more desirable.*

Time-out and spanking can be effective with younger children. Time-out is a method of discipline that separates the child from his environment and attention from others. When a four-year-old boy hits his two-year-old sister, he can be sent to a time-out chair in another room for a short period of time (no longer than five minutes) where he receives no attention. He is allowed to rejoin the family after he has sat quietly in the time-out chair for the specified period of time. (*Always* set a timer for a specific number of minutes so the child is not forgotten in time-out! Before I used a timer, I occasionally would forget my child was in time-out, until he would call, "Mom, can I come out now?") Quiet moments during time-out can be an unexpected treasure for a parent when children are small!

TO SPANK OR NOT TO SPANK?

Modern society criticizes spanking as a discipline method. Criticism is valid if spanking is administered for wrong reasons, harshly or incorrectly administered, or inconsistently given. Spanking, however, is biblical. Old Testament verses tell us not to despise chastening for God loves those he disciplines. "My son, do not despise the chastening of the Lord, nor detest His correction; For whom the Lord loves He corrects, just as a father the son in whom he delights" (Pr 3:11-12).

> *Wise parents use punishment as a corrective measure so that a child's spirit is not damaged and unconditional love is still given.*

Chasten means to correct and *improve* by means of punishment. Other Old Testament verses confirm the need for punishment:

- "Foolishness is bound up in the heart of a child, but the rod of correction will drive it far from him" (Pr 22:15).

- "The rod and reproof give wisdom, but a child left to *himself* brings shame to his mother" (Pr 29:15).

- "He who spares his rod hates his son, but he who loves him disciplines him promptly" (Pr 13:24).

Wise parents use punishment as a corrective measure so that a child's spirit is not damaged and unconditional love is still given. Improper punishment leads to destruction of a child's spirit and insecurity about parents' love. When my children were eight and nine years old, we witnessed a mother in a shopping mall spanking a child with her shoe and yelling at him at the same time. Her behavior was surely damaging to her child (and an unforgettable experience for my children who still recall the event!). Angry confrontations with children and youth in public places are damaging to relationships and to the child's self-esteem. *The goal of punishment and discipline is to control their will, not crush their spirit.*

> *Do not tolerate willful defiance. It may not seem so severe when children are young and offenses have small consequences.*

Old Testament Scriptures listed above describe punishment administered by a "rod," not by the hand. Why would a rod be used rather than a hand? What do parents do with their hands? Hands are used to administer love and care to a child by stroking, hugging and holding. It is more desirable to associate a hand with love rather than punishment. Therefore, a rod or other instrument is preferred for administering discipline. (Make sure the spanking instrument is kept away from children so they aren't tempted to hide it from parents!)

When Is Spanking Effective? In *The Strong-Willed Child*,[2] Dr. James Dobson states that spanking should only be used when a child is *willfully defiant*. What does that mean? *Willful defiance* is when a child *knowingly and willfully* does something the parent specifically told them in advance not to do *or* does not do something the parent specifically told them to do. When a child is willfully defiant, he must be confidently dealt with so the child knows that parents are the authority.

Do not tolerate willful defiance. It may not seem so severe when children are young and offenses have small consequences. Many adults laugh at little ones' disobedience. But small defiant children grow up to be defiant teenagers and adults who wreak havoc on families and society. A willfully defiant teen may stay out all night, drink, steal, take drugs, or get in trouble with the law. If respect and obedience to parents and laws of society have not been taught at an early age, parents won't be able to control defiant teenagers. Lack of discipline produces a lifestyle for families that can be equivalent to a "hell" on earth.

> *If respect and obedience to parents and laws of society have not been taught at an early age, parents won't be able to control defiant teenagers.*

My work involves dealing with families who have defiant and rebellious teenagers. Many times rebellion is a result of parents who have failed to establish good discipline practices when children were young, and who tolerate disobedience and disrespect. Lack of discipline and tolerance of disrespect will lead to rebellion. Parents will most likely deal with some rebellion during the adolescent years, so respect for authority should be established when children are young.

Willful Defiance or Childish Behavior? Distinguish between willful defiance and childish behavior. Spanking should only be used when children are willfully defiant—*purposefully disobeying parents' directives*. Childish behavior, on the other hand, may include spilling milk at the dinner table, forgetting to take out the trash, losing homework, staining their best clothes. Childish behavior should not be punished by spanking.

How should childish behaviors be managed? If a child spills milk, have him clean up the mess. Don't scold or yell. Calmly request that he clean it up. The child may be more careful the next time. When the trash is not taken out as instructed, request that the child take it out twice the following week (over-correction) or take it out earlier than necessary the next time.

How do parents respond to lost homework? Back up the teacher's punishment. The child may lose credit or have to stay in from recess to make up lost work. Talk to the teacher about a plan. Also, follow up at home to make sure homework is in the backpack before bedtime. Dealing with childish irresponsibility requires parents' involvement in teaching and rewarding appropriate behavior.

> *Children learn powerful lessons from natural consequences.*
>
> *Willful defiance must be dealt with in a firm, fair, and consistent manner.*

When a child stains his best clothes, have him try to remove the stain. If it doesn't come out, have him wear it anyway. When Melissa was seven years old, she talked her dad into buying her white satin dress shoes for Easter against my warnings about the difficulty of keeping them clean. When she got them muddy a few weeks after Easter and couldn't get them white and shiny again, she had to wear them anyway. After that incident, she never asked for white satin shoes again. Children learn powerful lessons from natural consequences.

What behaviors are considered willfully defiant? Willful defiance includes *refusing* to do a task when instructed by parents in a specified time period (e.g., pick up toys before going outside) or *doing* something expressly forbidden by parents (e.g., leaving the yard when told to stay in their own yard). These actions are committed with an "in your face" attitude. They beg for a response. Children want to know if parents are really in control. Willful defiance is their method of saying, "Show me you are really in charge!" Most families have at least one child who frequently tests the limits. Parents can draw a line of expected behavior that will be tolerated. Strong-willed children will have all ten toes on that line. Be on guard to keep children from stepping over the line. Willful defiance must be dealt with in a firm, fair, and consistent manner.

CHAPTER 10:

WHY IS DISCIPLINE NECESSARY?

Discipline is necessary in one respect because we must all live together in a civilized society that functions based on rules of appropriate behavior. From the beginning of mankind, disobedience has been a part of society. Can you imagine God having trouble with difficult children? Well, he did! Remember Adam and Eve? I found this reminder from the Internet (author unknown):

> After creating heaven and earth, God created Adam and Eve. And the first thing he said was, "Don't."
>
> "Don't what?" Adam replied.
>
> "Don't eat the forbidden fruit." God said.
>
> "Forbidden fruit? We have forbidden fruit? Hey, Eve . . . we have forbidden fruit!"
>
> "No way!"
>
> "Yes, way!"
>
> "Do NOT eat the fruit!" said God.
>
> "Why?"
>
> "Because I am your Father and I said so!" God replied, (wondering why he hadn't stopped creation after making the elephants).

A few minutes later, God saw His children having an apple break and was he ticked!

"Didn't I tell you not to eat the fruit?" God, as our first parent, asked.

"Uh-huh," Adam replied.

"Then why did you?" said the Father.

"I don't know," said Eve.

"She started it!" Adam said.

"Did not!"

"Did too!"

"Did not!"

Having had it with the two of them, God's punishment was that Adam and Eve should have children of their own. Thus, the pattern was set, and it has never changed! But there is reassurance in this story. If you have persistently and lovingly tried to give children wisdom and they haven't taken it, don't be hard on yourself. If God had trouble raising children, what makes you think it would be a piece of cake for you? Children today have free will just as God gave to Adam and Eve (and all of us!).

EFFECTIVE DISCIPLINE IS GOOD FOR KIDS

Effective discipline produces children with a healthy respect for others and themselves. Dr. Stanley Coopersmith, former associate professor of psychology at University of California-Davis, studied characteristics of 1700 pre-adolescent boys.[1] He found three important characteristics in homes that raised children with high self-esteem:

1. Highly esteemed children were more loved and appreciated.

2. Democracy and openness characterized their homes.

3. Parents of highly esteemed children were *stricter with discipline*. Parents demanded accountability, self control, and responsibility for behavior. Low-esteemed children, on the other side, lived in homes where permissiveness was prevalent. Rules weren't enforced. Children felt insecure because nobody seemed to care about them enough to enforce rules.

Effective discipline sends a message to children that parents love them and desire what is good for them. Discipline requires sacrifice for parents. Children appreciate the time and effort given to them for instruction and will, in most cases, respond positively.

> *Effective discipline sends a message to children that parents love them and desire what is good for them.*

RESPECT FOR AUTHORITY

Discipline is also necessary for children to develop an understanding that Christians live under the authority of God. Parents are the child's first authority. When children learn to respect and trust parents, they will better understand their relationship with God and submit to His authority. Do not tolerate disrespect from children.

In my own practice, I have witnessed teenagers and children who were openly disrespectful to parents, telling them to "shut-up", demanding money, car keys and even young men demanding their girlfriends being allowed to spend the night in the parents' home!

These disrespectful and disobedient adolescents will have difficulty maintaining appropriate relationships with family and friends, keeping a job, and excelling in society. They have no respect for authority and as a result are not very teachable.

81

MODELING SELF-DISCIPLINE

Adults must be the role model for a disciplined lifestyle. When parents submit to the discipline (teaching and correction) of the Heavenly Father, children will more likely submit to discipline and authority of parents and God.

What does God do when His children disobey Him? He disciplines them. "As many as I love, I rebuke and chasten. Therefore be zealous and repent" (Re 3:19). "If you endure chastening, God deals with you as with sons; for what son is there whom a father does not chasten? But if you are without chastening, of which all have become partakers, then you are illegitimate and not sons" (He 12:7-8).

> *Discipline conveys respect, value, and high esteem.*

Why does God discipline His children when they do wrong? Because He *loves* them. Therefore, parents should discipline children because *they* love them. Discipline conveys respect, value, and high esteem. I remember my dad saying just before he punished me, "this hurts me more than it does you". At the time, that did not make sense to me. But as a parent, I understand now what he meant.

Discipline, like most behavior, is "caught" rather than "taught." When children see the fruits of their parents' disciplined lifestyle, they will desire to follow in their footsteps. They will most likely cling to good and hate evil. As Romans 12:9 states, "Let love be without hypocrisy. Abhor what is evil. Cling to what is good." Parents must model the desired behaviors and discourage undesirable behaviors. How? Have good eating habits and discourage gluttony, exercise regularly, display good sleep habits, use positive talk (no foul language or constant criticism!), be honest, trustworthy and compassionate, admit wrong, show unconditional love, be prompt (to work, church, and appointments with children), and get along with others. Parenting isn't easy! Children are willing to forgive parents' mistakes but they must see a consistent *effort* to model good behaviors.

Parents will take this seriously when they begin to see their behaviors mirrored in their children. I had a friend recently who said her daughter called from another city after a visit to her parents' home and asked, "Did Dad teach Jessie how to turn his cereal bowl up, drink milk from the bowl, and then make a loud 'ahhhh' sound when finished?" My friend said she held her laughter in check when she answered her daughter with a sorrowful sounding "yes". Talk to any teacher and he will be full of stories about what children mimic from their parents!

The goal of teaching discipline is *self*-discipline. Productive and successful adults must be self-disciplined and respect authority. It is the job of parents to teach discipline and respect. Parents train out of love with an attitude of correcting and restoring the relationship. That's the only way discipline is effective. When parents punish out of anger rather than love, discipline is less effective. Children are *discouraged* rather than *encouraged* to do right. "Fathers, do not provoke your children, lest they become discouraged" (Col 3:21). "And you, fathers, do not provoke your children to wrath, but bring them up in the training and admonition of the Lord" (Ep 6:4).

> *Children are willing to forgive parents' mistakes but they must see a consistent effort to model good behaviors.*

WHY CHILDREN MISBEHAVE

Five-year-old Joey ran into my office recently and headed straight for my computer. He sat in *my* chair, and his little fingers began dancing on my keyboard as he asked, "What kind of games do you have?" After shutting down the computer and listening to Joey complain, I tried to engage him in another activity. During the therapy hour, he did not sit for more than five minutes without getting out of his chair and into mischief. Verbal commands went in one ear and out the other (if they went in at all!). Each time I needed Joey to perform a task, I had to leave my chair and physically guide Joey back to his. After an hour of battling the wills, I thought, "How does his mom live with this rambunctious ball of energy everyday?" (Actually, the reason he was in my office was to evaluate him because mom could not control his behavior.)

No parent raises a perfect child. Some are easier than others to guide and train. That is why discipline is necessary. Why do children misbehave anyway? Don't they realize life would be much easier for them (and parents!) if they would mind? What is their motivation for misbehavior?

Don Dinkmeyer and Gary D. McKay, in *STEP-Systematic Training for Effective Parenting: The Parent's Handbook*,[2] explains four mistaken goals for misbehavior: Attention, Power, Revenge, and Assumed Inadequacy.

Attention. Some children misbehave to get attention. They are saying, "I only belong when I have your attention." Because children get attention from parents when they misbehave, misbehavior is reinforced. Children will accept negative attention over *no* attention. When children misbehave, parents should ask, "Is he seeking my attention? Have we not been giving this child enough positive attention?" Loss of attention may occur when a new baby is born, Mom takes a job outside the home, work takes a parent out of town frequently, or families experience any type of stressful situation that changes the daily functioning of a family. Focus on giving the child more positive attention.

If parents can pinpoint a lack of attention as the reason for misconduct, make sure that positive attention is directed to the child. Depending on the child's age and maturity, it may be appropriate to talk to the child about his attention needs and the parents' failure to meet them. Apologize for being distracted by other tasks or people and assure the child of your love and renewed attention. Spend more time with the child offering positive attention.

Power. Power is another motivation behind misbehavior. Some children think they must always win the battles, or at least not allow parents to win, in order to feel they belong. Engaging in power struggles with children only intensifies discord. "Pulling Mom's strings" is a behavior easily learned. For example, frequent battles over what is for breakfast is a power struggle between parent and child that is often won by the child because the parent feels guilty when the child doesn't eat or goes to school emotionally upset.

If children cannot win a battle in one matter, they may exert power in another area, such as refusing to do homework. For example, if a child is angry because he wasn't allowed to spend the night out at a friend's house the previous weekend, he may show his power by not doing homework. Determine if there has been a conflict in another matter that could be the cause of a power struggle. Recognize power struggles and do not engage with the child.

Revenge. Misconduct occurs sometimes because children seek revenge. Children may not feel a sense of belonging and will try to "get back" at parents through misbehavior, with the intent of hurting parents. This is common in divorce situations where children feel they have lost their sense of belonging in a family and will act out to punish parents. They may be angry or hurt because a parent has moved out of the home, doesn't keep them on certain weekends, or has died. Children will misbehave to seek revenge against parents. Revenge may also occur with children who are angry or hurt over an issue, such as not being allowed to go out for an evening with friends or purchase a desired toy.

A young man in therapy recently used revenge to get back at his parents. Dad was in prison. Mom had moved to another state with a drug-addicted boyfriend. He lived with his grandmother who did not seem to have control over his behavior. This young man stayed in trouble with the police and couldn't keep a steady job. Through therapy, motivation for his misconduct and his need for a loving family unit were revealed. He was able to learn positive ways to express needs.

Assumed Inadequacy. Some children misbehave because they feel inadequate and inferior. Belief in who they are and what they can achieve has not been instilled. Therefore, they "give up" trying to do the right thing and revert to misbehavior. A young woman recently told me that her mom never encouraged her and told her she would end up just like her dad (who was in prison). Parental responsibility includes teaching and nurturing. When children feel secure, better behavior is usually noted. They may turn misbehavior outward through tantrums, disobeying rules and laws, and becoming aggressive or physically abusive. Misconduct turned inward may result in depression and withdrawal, not making an effort at school or other activities, drug/alcohol abuse or abuse regarding their own physical need for food, hygiene, and sleep. Children must be stimulated and encouraged to perform to ensure experiencing success. Helping children believe in themselves and their value to society will reduce this need to act out. (See Part I on building self-esteem.)

BELONGING AND SIGNIFICANCE

The main goal of *all* behavior is to discover a sense of belonging and significance. A sense of inadequacy leads children to seek negative attention, engage in power struggles, seek revenge, and give up on trying to behave appropriately. Children assume that attention or power will help them achieve significance. Revenge, they assert, will give some satisfaction for hurt caused by not feeling they belong. Assumed inadequacy is like the fear of failure. If they don't try, they don't have to worry about failing.

IDENTIFYING INAPPROPRIATE GOALS OF MISBEHAVIOR

Why do parents need to identify inappropriate goals of misbehavior? Misbehavior is a *symptom* of problems, much like a fever is a symptom of illness. Therefore, to correct misconduct, a diagnosis must be made. Discover the "inappropriate" goal in order to change the behavior. Children can't always pinpoint what they need. Parents must help discover true goals of misbehavior so that needs are met appropriately.

> *The main goal of all behavior is to discover a sense of belonging and significance.*
>
> *Misbehavior is a symptom of problems, much like a fever is a symptom of illness.*

When children misbehave, the goal may be any four of the mistaken goals of misbehavior: attention, revenge, power, or assumed inadequacy. To identify the inappropriate goal, look at the common characteristics for each goal and ask if this could be the cause of misbehavior. Does he need attention? Is this a power struggle? Could revenge be a motivator? Does my child feel inadequate? Once identified, appropriate steps described can be applied to eliminate undesirable behavior.

REACTING TO MISBEHAVIOR

Once a misdirected behavior goal is identified (in other words, the reason for misbehavior), parents can learn how to meet the needs of children and change their misbehavior by eliminating the problem. If attention is the goal, focus attention on children when they are behaving in an *acceptable* way. Ignore misbehavior (if possible). Plan special times to do things together. Use praise liberally. Rather than giving negative attention, allow logical consequences to occur. For example, the morning breakfast struggle can be eliminated by giving a choice between two items for the meal. The child can choose *which* of the two he would like for breakfast. This gives the child control (within limits) that is acceptable to the parents. If the child doesn't choose an option, allow him to go to school without breakfast. The hunger pangs he will feel about mid-morning will assure him that he should make a breakfast choice the next morning!

When power is the motivation, *back off!* Do not engage in power struggles with children, if at all possible. Again, allow logical consequences to occur. Follow up confrontation with a problem solving plan. For example, "If you complete the homework assignment, I'll give you a special treat or allow a special activity." Negotiate. Offer an incentive. Elicit their cooperation. It becomes a win/win situation. If the child continues to refuse to complete homework, then entertainment activities can be withheld. Punishment will be administered by the teacher. In the end, parents have the ultimate control.

When children are very small, it may be important to demonstrate to children the appropriate behavior and not allow defiant behavior. I witnessed a good example of this situation recently at the post office. As I stood in an endless line at the service counter, I was entertained by two young children who had discovered a basket of collector stamp books. Big sister was "reading" the books to little brother while mom was collecting a package. When mom finished and said, "Let's go, children," Big Sister began to leave with the stamp book in hand. Mom said, "Honey, you can't take the book with you. Leave the book." An emphatic "no," was Big Sister's reply. After several unsuccessful verbal enticements from Mom to leave the book, Mom finally walked over to Big Sister and (after a struggle!) took the book away. Then mom began to walk out the door with Little Brother without ever looking back to see if Big Sister was following her. Reluctantly, and with folded arms and puffy cheeks, Big Sister followed. When they finally got out the door, Big Sister reached up to Mom with both arms open wide wanting to be held. Mom gently picked her up and held her close. Mom realized the verbal reprimands were a power struggle she could not win and finally had to physically take the book away. This works with little ones but is not as successful with kids who are bigger than you!

Retaliation is a natural behavior in response to revenge. Don't be tempted to retaliate, and don't provoke children even when they provoke parents. Revenge has a snowballing effect that can produce irreparable damage to the family unit. One bad behavior leads to another. Teens can retaliate with behaviors that have life long consequences (drugs, automobile accidents, alcohol abuse, pregnancy). Spend time with the child. Decide on needs. Encourage and problem-solve together.

Dealing with inadequacy gives parents an opportunity to assess children's abilities and weaknesses and teach desired skills and behavior. Help children learn a task. Encourage success and effort. Setting incremental goals and achieving them gives children a can-do attitude. Teach them simple chores around the house. Praise them for completing a job. This ensures self-confidence and self-worth. If a child is not doing homework, make sure the child *can* perform the task.

Talk to the teacher. Engage a tutor. Help with homework. If that doesn't solve the homework problem, have him evaluated by a qualified examiner to eliminate the possibility of a learning disability and/or attention problems.

Reacting appropriately to misbehavior goals will eliminate need for misbehavior. Meeting needs of belonging and self-worth will reduce likelihood of persistent conduct problems.

> *Reacting appropriately to misbehavior goals will eliminate need for misbehavior.*

CHAPTER 11:

SPECIFIC GUIDELINES OF DISCIPLINE

Implementing effective discipline requires many parameters. Each child responds to different types of discipline based on their own temperaments. Specific guidelines for discipline are needed regardless of the type of teaching and/or correction. This chapter outlines ideas that will help make discipline effective.

DEFINE BOUNDARIES

Children need to know what behavior is expected. Define boundaries in advance so children know what is acceptable and what is not. Punishing children for behavior that they did not know was wrong is an injustice to children and will lead to mistrust of parents. Children need fair and concise guidelines. Specific goals for behavior should be clearly communicated. Discuss expected behavior in advance. If you expect your child to be home at 5:00 p.m. from playing in the

> *Define boundaries in advance so children know what is acceptable and what is not.*

neighborhood, be specific in discussing the rule. Say, "If you come in from playing by 5:00 p.m., then you may go out to play again tomorrow. If you come in from playing *after* 5:00 p.m., you won't be able to play outside tomorrow. I want you to be inside the house by 5:00. Do you have your watch on?

Do you know what time 5:00 is? Look at me. Tell me what I just said. Do you understand?" Discipline is effective when the rules are clearly understood.

LOGICAL CONSEQUENCES

When appropriate, allow logical consequences to occur. Children can learn appropriate behavior from logical consequences so that *parents are not always the controlling factor*. Children learn that behavior has other consequences besides their parents' displeasure. When consequences are experienced, children learn to control actions and *think* about reactions their behavior may cause. For example, children can learn, "If I don't eat breakfast, I may get hungry at school." "If I don't put dirty clothes in the laundry basket, clothes won't be washed and I won't have clean clothes to wear." (This only works with kids who care about being clean!)

> *Children can learn appropriate behavior from logical consequences so that parents are not always the controlling factor.*

APPROPRIATE EXPECTATIONS

Before asking children to perform a task, make sure they know how to do the job. Teach them specifically what is expected. Be sure the task is within their ability to perform. Asking a six-year-old to clean the kitchen may result in only dishes being stacked in the sink and food put away in the refrigerator. Requesting the same task from a teenager should result in much more effort.

After the ability is established, be specific about expectations. When asking children to clean the kitchen, what specific tasks are involved? Washing dishes or loading the dishwasher? Putting away leftover food? Cleaning the stove? Wiping the counter tops? Sweeping the floor? Make a list of specific tasks until children have learned what is required to complete a job to Mom's satisfaction.

IDENTIFY APPROPRIATE LIMITS

Limits are an aspect of life that we all experience: speed limits, cash withdrawal limits, IRA contribution limits, charge card limits, and vacation and sick day restrictions. Children need to know limits. They find security in knowing and living within limits. Remember the story abut the fourteen-year-old girl who didn't have limits? Children may never admit it, but they want to know the boundaries. They are assured of their parents' love when they have reasonable and consistent boundaries. Total freedom can be frightening to a child (even a teenager, but most will not admit it!).

Recent studies show that the part of a teenager's brain (pre-frontal cortex) involving moral judgment and decision making is not fully developed until the early- or mid-twenties.

Recent studies show that the part of a teenager's brain (pre-frontal cortex) involving moral judgment and decision making is not fully developed until the early- or mid-twenties. This discovery can be influential in helping teens understand why certain limits are necessary. One teenage girl I know was glad her mom didn't let her go to the beach unchaperoned during spring break, even though she cried and pouted about not going. She later told her mom she wasn't sure of making that decision herself because of temptations that could occur with a group of teens away from home and parental supervision.

Children and teens are more comfortable and secure with a degree of freedom within reasonable limits. A seven-year-old may want to choose what to wear for a special occasion. Give her a choice of three appropriate dresses. A preteen may want to choose a fun activity on Saturday night. Allow him to choose from a parent-approved list.

As children mature, boundaries change. Just as they outgrow clothes from year to year, boundaries must be expanded. Discuss these with children. Agree on new limits as long as responsible behavior is exhibited by the child. Sometimes, teens will challenge limits to see if parents will really uphold them. They may not *really* want more freedom but are testing parents' boundaries. A parent may hear, "David's parents let him stay out until 1 a.m. on weekends. Why can't I?" The teen may not want to have a 1 a.m. curfew but may be testing a parent's limits. Keep in mind, too, that asking David's parents about his curfew may yield a different story than the one David told! Be fair and consistent. Teenagers need limits within reason, even if they appear to be rebellious or resistant. They may verbalize that the rules are too strict. But most are accepting and obedient when rules are fair and reasonable.

> *Teenagers need limits within reason, even if they appear to be rebellious or resistant.*

BE CONSISTENT

Consistency in enforcing boundaries helps children feel safe. Children need to know the boundaries and be assured that parents will enforce them consistently. Be firm with rules and limits. Inconsistency is unfair and confusing. Parents know how inconsistency feels at work when rules and expectations are enforced for some workers but not others, or when rules are constantly changing. Children feel the same. Inconsistency makes them sense that parents may not be trusted because they don't know when rules will be enforced. Insecurity is felt because children don't know if or when boundaries will change.

For example, if a child has problems with hitting other children, a parent must be consistent in dealing with behavior *whenever* and *wherever* it occurs. If a parent punishes hitting behavior at the park with other children but ignores it at home with siblings, the child learns that the "no hitting" rules are not steadfast. It is allowed in some situations but not others. Hitting is tolerated at home as long as nobody outside the family sees, but not permitted in social settings.

PRIVACY, PLEASE

The negative discipline required with children should only occur in private. Whether it is a verbal reprimand or a physical punishment, *always* do it in private. No one else should see or hear parents discipline children. Such public displays crush children's spirits by demeaning them in front of others and showing disrespect.

Recently, a mother gave her small child a verbal lashing that caused me to blush with embarrassment. This mother scolded her child in a doctor's waiting room full of patients watching. Such behavior is totally inappropriate and does a child more harm than good. When discipline is necessary in a public place, such as an office, grocery store, or mall, find a restroom or go to the car to deal with the child in private. After punishment is administered or spoken, hold that child close. Assure him of love. Talk to him in a soft tone about the wrong behavior. Tell him what behavior is expected. *The purpose of discipline is restoration.* Children need to know they are loved, and because they are loved, parents cannot allow misconduct.

DISCIPLINE WITHOUT ANGER

A healthy fear and respect for parents is desired. Just as Christians obey God out of respect and fear of His judgment, because He is a just God, children should fear and respect parents. Healthy fear and respect are based on consistent and fair discipline methods. Unhealthy fear and disrespect are born out of punishment that is erratic and filled with anger. Effective discipline requires parents to deal with children without yelling, screaming, hitting, or throwing a temper tantrum. In Proverbs 15:1 we read "A soft answer turns away wrath." When parents yell or display anger, credibility and respect are lost. A normal tone of voice must be maintained. Good eye contact is necessary. Make an effort to listen to children (regardless of the absurdity of their excuse). If a parent is emotionally out of control, discipline should be postponed or dealt with by the other parent. Never discipline children when anger can't be controlled.

> *Discipline and guidance may be rejected when anger is involved in punishment.*

Discipline and guidance may be rejected when anger is involved in punishment. Children react to the *anger* of parents rather than the reason for discipline. They don't see beyond their parents' reaction. When a teenager makes a disrespectful comment to his mother and the mother reacts with a yelling temper tantrum, the teen only reacts to the mother's irrational tantrum and can't see his own mistake of being disrespectful to his mother. The parent's reaction is sometimes worse than the teen's offense and doesn't become a teaching experience.

I tell you this by experience! When my twenty-year-old college student was home for Christmas holidays last year, she and I were having a "discussion" as I was clearing out the dishwasher. She made a very disrespectful remark to me (which I do not tolerate well!). My first reaction was to throw something at her—which I did! Thankfully, I had a plastic container in my hand instead of a glass coffee mug! *My reaction was worse than her disrespectful comment!* I had to apologize to her first. To this day, I don't remember what the disrespectful remark was that rolled off her tongue. But I will always remember the look on her face when the plastic bowl landed at her feet!

Respect and trust are conveyed only when emotions are controlled. If discipline can't be done without anger, allow a cooling off period before confronting a child or allow the other parent to deal with the situation. Recently, while shopping in a department store, I witnessed a heated conversation between a teenage daughter and mother. Both were talking loud enough to draw attention to themselves in the middle of the sportswear department! I wanted to go over and say, "Hey, let's call a truce. You are making a scene!" But this was not my right! Mom would probably have yelled at me for interfering. Confrontational scenes in public do not build trust or respect. Shopping with teenage girls is an emotionally charged experience that can be minimized by deciding together on some rules in advance of shopping—spending limits, guidelines for appropriate clothing, and certain stores to shop.

> *Respect and trust are conveyed only when emotions are controlled.*

PICK YOUR BATTLES

Focus on issues that really matter. Try not to nag children about every little thing. Pick and choose battles. Parents will have much more credibility when not constantly nagging. When parents must say "no" about an issue, children will be more likely to accept a negative response because they experience "yes" more often and aren't consistently being told "no."

Give children the freedom to make choices when appropriate. Freedom gives them responsibility and gives them power over their own lives. If children load the dishwasher in a different way from parents, that's okay as long as dishes get clean. If spending weekly allowance in one day is their choice, so what? They will learn by logical consequences. When they want an ice cream cone at the end of the week but don't have the money, they will understand why parents suggest that they don't spend their allowance in one day. If a ten-year-old wants to wear a bra, even though she doesn't physically need it, who does it hurt? Pick the important battles and stand firm. Let go of little things that may annoy you and focus on the important battles.

LIGHTEN UP

Use humor when children make mistakes. Teach them to laugh at themselves. Not every mistake is a catastrophe.

> *Let go of little things that may annoy you and focus on the important battles.*

Children will act like children. They will do childish things, such as spill drinks, forget chores, leave clothes on the floor, say things they shouldn't.

My dear friend, Joy, sings (not so much on key, either) a particular song when she wants her son to pick up his shoes left on the den floor. He picks them up when he hears her sing, "This is the way we pick up our shoes, pick up our shoes, pick up our shoes"! It has become a joke between them.

At family gatherings when children were young, our daughter, Melissa, and her girl cousins, would perform skits for the family depicting funny events or actions of each family member. After the girls' skits, aunts and uncles would reciprocate with skits about the girls. All had a big laugh!

REASONABLE DISCIPLINE

Make the punishment fit the crime. Be reasonable. Unreasonable and excessive punishment doesn't teach appropriate behavior. Children become bitter, angry, and insecure. Punishment should be severe enough to prevent behavior from occurring again but not so excessive that there is no hope for success in the future.

Recently, a mom told me that her son stayed gone from home too long one Saturday playing with friends in the neighborhood. She told him when he got home that he would be grounded for a month. No television. No video games. No computer. No playing outside. I suggested the punishment was unreasonable and too severe. I asked her what she would do if he misbehaved in some other way during the next month. What could she take away that hasn't already been eliminated? What incentive is left for the child to behave appropriately? A more appropriate punishment, I suggested, would be to require him to play in his own yard the next Saturday. If his friends didn't want to play in his yard, then he would have to play alone.

> *Positive and productive attitudes that encourage success should be taught just as appropriate behaviors are taught.*

Make sure the punishment doesn't punish the parent more than child! Can you imagine entertaining a twelve-year-old for a month without media entertainment or allowing him out of the yard?!

ATTITUDE ADJUSTMENT

Deal with bad attitudes as severely as bad behaviors. Children aren't born with perfect attitudes any more than they are born with perfect behavior. (Remember those crying babies and difficult toddlers!) Positive and productive *attitudes* that encourage success should be taught just as appropriate *behaviors* are taught. Teach children respect, honor, trust, compassion, selflessness, love, and positive thinking. Teaching desirable attitudes is as important as teaching desirable behaviors. One bad apple *can* spoil the whole basket! In other words, one negative child can affect the family's home environment. Deal with negative attitudes. Help children discover the cause of the negative attitude and how to change to positive attitudes.

A common experience in family life is children who come home from school after a difficult day with a bad attitude. Take time to talk about the day. What happened at school that might have caused a negative mood? Try to identify problems. Did the teacher yell at the child? Was there a fight with a friend? Did he make a bad grade on a test? Seek a solution to the problem. If the problem can't be identified, ask the child to stop the negative attitude or go to his room until he can join the family with a better attitude. This worked with my children when they were young. After a short period of time, they would come out of their room. I would ask for a smile. When they smiled at me, I would smile back and give them a big hug and kiss. Attitudes change. Positive experiences follow good attitudes.

Practice saying positive things to children. Sometimes positive *actions* will produce positive *attitudes*. "You did a great job eating all your dinner." "You put away all the toys!" "A bath makes you smell so clean." Just like adults *must* do things they don't want to do, teach children that sometimes the action comes first and the attitude follows. Actions can be required of children regardless of the attitude. Actions encourage a change in behavior. The attitude will likely follow. The child may think to himself, "Mom likes it when I pick up toys, . . . eat all my dinner, . . . take a bath."

TEACH AND REINFORCE

To eliminate a negative behavior, children must be taught an appropriate behavior to replace the negative. Teach children behaviors that are appropriate and expected. Reinforce positive behaviors with verbal praise, a pat on the back, or a tangible reward (lunch at a favorite restaurant or the purchase of a special toy). Positive reinforcement encourages the child to continue the behavior. Reinforce positive attitudes as well as behaviors! "I like the happy face you wore today while shopping with me. Would you like to stop for ice cream before going home?"

SEPARATE THE CHILD FROM THE BEHAVIOR

Many times I hear parents say to children, "You're a bad boy!" like they were talking to an animal! Telling children they are bad lowers self expectation and convinces them they are bad. Why should they try to be good if parents tell them they are bad?

Separate the undesirable behavior from the worth of the child. When disciplining children, be specific about unacceptable behavior. Let them know that the *behavior* is not acceptable. Don't reject the child. Instead of saying, "You're a bad boy", say, "Hitting is an unacceptable behavior. You're a good boy and good boys don't hit." This pinpoints a specific behavior but doesn't discourage the child. The child will think, *Mom believes I am a good boy. I should act like a good boy.* Remember, children are like wet cement. Self-worth is dependent on what parents believe and express about the child. The child will become what parents think of them. Reaffirming good behavior raises self expectations.

> *Separate the undesirable behavior from the worth of the child.*

Reassure children of love, and *because* of love, parents cannot allow misbehavior. When parents say, "I love you, but . . . ," they are putting conditions on love. When dealing with misconduct say, "I love you, *and* because I love you, I cannot accept this conduct."

DISCIPLINE WITH GRACE

Parenting is a tough job. Parents aren't perfect. They will make mistakes. (Remember my story about the plastic bowl?) Err on the side of grace, if unsure about appropriate discipline. Children learn about God's love and grace through their relationship with parents. When parents show unconditional love and grace to children, it encourages them. They can understand God's desire for a relationship with them. Harsh and unfair punishment discourages children.

For example, if a child is grounded for the weekend but has a special event (birthday party, etc.) they had planned to attend, consider making an exception for a few hours to allow them to go. Explain the reason for suspension of the grounding. Let them know parents believe a lesson has been learned from the mistake and want to show love and forgiveness the way God loves and forgives us. Children may learn a more valuable lesson about God's love and grace!

> *Children learn about God's love and grace through their relationship with parents.*

Grace and forgiveness are also learned by children when parents admit mistakes. When you make a mistake in disciplining your child, say "I am sorry. I made a mistake." Ask forgiveness. Children are the most forgiving people in the world when they sense a parent's sincerity. Let them see that parents are willing to admit mistakes. They will learn to trust and be more likely to admit when they are wrong.

WHAT KIND OF DISCIPLINE WORKS?

No two children are alike. Ask any parent who has more than one child. What works with disciplining one child may not work with another. Try various methods of discipline and learn what works best with each child. Reasoning and talking through problems worked extremely well with one of my children. The other (who will remain anonymous!) required specific rules and parents who were willing to enforce them. The limits were always being tested. The toes were always on the line!

The goal of discipline is to shape a child's will and protect his spirit. Parents must address the need for discipline and, at the same time, build self-esteem. Security is encouraged when children know rules and are assured parents will consistently enforce them. Fair and reasonable discipline encourages children.

Logical consequences and teaching desired behavior are best methods of discipline. Logical consequences teach new behaviors so that negative consequences are avoided. Logical and natural consequences are learned throughout life. Speeding will result in a traffic ticket. Overeating will result in weight gain. Smoking will lead to poor health. Unexcused absences will lead to job loss. Teaching children to consider consequences of behavior will encourage thinking skills and responsibility for their own actions.

> *Logical consequences and teaching desired behavior are best methods of discipline.*

Many times after seeing that lonely brown bag lunch left on the kitchen counter, I wanted to jump in the car and lovingly deliver it to my child at school! And I did that a few times in the early school days, but then realized the child wasn't concerned about forgotten lunches because he could count on mom to special deliver it to him. When I stopped delivering left-at-home lunches to school, my children made sure they didn't leave home without that brown paper bag. Hunger is an excellent motivator! I didn't have to nag, and I wasn't to blame if lunches were left at home.

Taking time to teach appropriate behavior to children gives them self-confidence and the ability to control their own lives (which is the long-term goal of parenting). When they learn to be responsible for their attitudes and behaviors, children will have confidence to tackle new challenges and be willing to seek parents' advice and instruction.

Negative punishment should be reserved for willful defiance. Spanking should not be administered after about age nine or ten. Other punishment is preferable because children can then understand right and wrong and consequences of behavior. Some children are never or rarely spanked because they want to please parents. They are compliant children. (Thank God for compliant children!) Others keep all ten toes on the line drawn for them and dare parents to do something about it! Don't retreat. When those toes step over the line, deal with them confidently and with determination. Control must be established with young children to discourage rebellion in the sometimes difficult teen years. Mistakes teenagers make can be life-altering to them and to the families that have to pick up the pieces.

> *When those toes step over the line, deal with them confidently and with determination.*

CHAPTER 12:

RESULTS OF EFFECTIVE DISCIPLINE

April 20, 1999, is a date that will be long remembered because of the tragic shootings in Littleton, Colorado, of fifteen people at a local high school. Innocent students and a teacher were brutally gunned down by two classmates who turned the guns on themselves after their savage shooting spree.

One of their victims was a young girl named Cassie Bernall. Her story of confidently admitting to her assailant that she was a Christian has made her a modern day martyr. *She Said Yes, The Unlikely Martyrdom of Cassie Bernall*, written by her mother (Misty Bernall) after her death, has been widely read.

Cassie would not likely have been a respected Christian young lady had it not been for the disciplinary stance taken by her parents just three years prior to her untimely death. In their book, interviews, and magazine articles, Cassie's mother, Misty, chronicles the events that led to Cassie becoming a Christian. Three years prior to the shootings, Misty found in Cassie's room disturbing notes that contained graphic sexual language, gruesome drawings of axes, knives, and vampire teeth embedded in bodies, along with other evidences of demonic worship.

Shocking death threats against a teacher and threats against her parents were also found in the notes.

Misty had felt a growing distance in her relationship with Cassie, but had no idea Cassie had developed an interest in witchcraft, self-mutilation, drugs, and alcohol. After contacting police, their pastor, and the parents of Cassie's friend who wrote some of the notes, the Bernall's confronted Cassie. She responded with anger and rage. As the Bernall's set down new rules for Cassie, that included no contact with her former friends, she rebelled and threatened to run away and commit suicide.

Cassie's father, Brad, recalls the difficult days of dealing with Cassie's anger and rebellion.[1] "There were times when she was acting so irrationally that we felt like slapping her, just to knock her back to her senses. But I never did. Instead I put my arms around her even tighter, pulled her close, and said over and over, 'I love you, Cassie and I don't want to see you do anything to hurt yourself. I don't want to see anything bad happen to you at all.'"

The parents were persistent in their fight for Cassie's life. They transferred her to a private Christian high school. They began random searches of her room, monitored phone calls, and kept track of where she went and with whom she associated. No contact with old friends was allowed. Prayer was constant.

Cassie's mom said, "In a way, it is the hardest thing you can ever do as parents: to put your foot down and say, 'this stops right here.'" Eventually, their persistence paid off with Cassie. In the spring of 1997, Cassie was allowed to attend a church youth retreat. That weekend provided an opportunity for Cassie to make a life-changing decision. She accepted Jesus Christ as her Lord and Savior. Her decision was evident in her life from that moment until the day she claimed eternal life and said, "Yes, I believe," to two teenage gunmen who killed her and twelve others at Columbine High.

Cassie's life was saved by the persistent and loving discipline of two courageous parents. Misty Bernall says, "If I've learned anything from Cassie's short life, it is that no adolescent, however rebellious, is doomed by fate. With warmth, self-sacrifice, and honesty—with the love that ultimately comes from God—every child can be guided and saved. . . . I think there is hope for every kid that is in trouble. You can step in and help them turn their lives around."

The Bernalls' courageous and persistent discipline of their daughter is a dramatic example of the results of effective discipline. Hopefully, with good parenting skills, most parents won't face the Bernalls' challenge. Proverbs 22:6 states, "Train up a child in the way he should go, and when he is old he will not depart from it." The verse doesn't mean kids won't make mistakes, but most will return to parents' training. Appropriate and effective discipline is a necessary part of teaching children. It provides a positive lifelong relationship between parents and children. "Correct your son, and he will give you rest; Yes, he will give delight to your soul" (Pr 29:17). Children will appreciate and respect a sincere effort of good parenting and desire a lifelong relationship with parents.

> *Lifelong honor and respect will be earned for parents who have successfully disciplined children.*

Raising disciplined and respectful children is a positive contribution to society. Children will have keys to success in careers and raising families of their own. The torch will be passed to a new generation of parents. Discipline is teaching children how to live. Self-discipline is the goal. Lifelong honor and respect will be earned for parents who have successfully disciplined children.

From the Internet (author unknown), I found what I believe sums up the importance of discipline and training:

I LOVED YOU ENOUGH

Someday when my children are old enough to understand the logic that motivates a parent, I will tell them:

I loved you enough . . . to ask where you were going,

With whom, and what time you would be home.

I loved you enough . . . to insist that you save your money and buy things for yourself even though I could afford to buy them for you.

I loved you enough . . . to be silent and let you discover that your new best friend was a creep.

I loved you enough . . . to make you go pay for the bubble gum you had taken and tell the clerk, "I stole this yesterday and want to pay for it."

I loved you enough . . . to stand over you for two hours while you cleaned your room, a job that should have taken 15 minutes.

I loved you enough . . . to let you see anger, disappointment, and tears in my eyes.

Children must learn that their parents aren't perfect.

I loved you enough . . . to let you assume the responsibility for your actions even when the penalties were so harsh they almost broke my heart.

But most of all, I loved you enough . . . to say NO when I knew you would hate me for it.

Those were the most difficult battles of all. I'm glad I won them, because in the end you won, too. And someday when your children are old enough to understand the logic that motivates parents, you will tell them . . .

Was your mom mean? I know mine was. We had the meanest mother in the whole world! While other kids ate candy for breakfast, we had to have cereal, eggs, and toast.

When others had a Pepsi and a Twinkie for lunch, we had to eat sandwiches. And you can guess our mother fixed us a dinner that was different from what other kids had, too.

Mother insisted on knowing where we were at all times.

You'd think we were convicts in a prison. She had to know who our friends were and what we were doing with them. She insisted that if we said we would be gone for an hour, we would be gone for an hour or less. We were ashamed to admit it, but she had the nerve to break the Child Labor Laws by making us work. We had to wash dishes, make the beds, learn to cook, vacuum the floor, do laundry, empty the trash and all sorts of cruel jobs. I think she would lie awake at night thinking of more things for us to do. She always insisted on us telling the truth, the whole truth, and nothing but the truth. By the time we were teenagers, she could read our minds. Then, life was really tough! Mother wouldn't let our friends just honk the horn when they drove up. They had to come up to the door so she could meet them. While everyone else could date when they were 12 or 13, we had to wait until we were 16. Because of our mother, we missed out on lots of things other kids experienced.

None of us has ever been caught shoplifting, vandalizing other's property, or even arrested for any crime. It was all her fault. Now that we have left home, we are all educated, honest adults. We are doing our best to be mean parents just like Mom was. I think that is what's wrong with the world today. It just doesn't have enough mean moms.

SUMMARY

Effective discipline and training is an important task for parents that requires understanding the motives of misbehavior, the need for discipline, and effective ways to teach children. Specific guidelines for discipline include: defining boundaries, allowing logical consequences to occur, teaching appropriate expectations, identifying appropriate limits, striving for consistency, assuring a need for privacy in discipline, disciplining without anger, choosing battles, using humor, being reasonable, dealing with attitudes, reinforcing desired behaviors, separating behaviors from the worth of the child, and disciplining with grace. Effective discipline methods depend on the personality of the child. The goal of discipline is to teach self-discipline and responsibility so that children can grow up to be responsible and respectful adults.

PART IV

KIDS AND CASH: TEACHING CHILDREN HOW TO MANAGE MONEY

CHAPTER 13:

MONEY MATTERS!

"SHOW ME THE MONEY!" is a saying made famous by the hit movie, *Jerry McGuire*, starring Tom Cruise and Cuba Gooding, Jr. "Show me the money!" Yes, money keeps the economy growing and the investment markets moving. Money pays for gasoline, mortgages, groceries, clothes, and all the zillion things consumers buy each year. Whether you pay cash, write a check, use a debit card, transfer from an online banking service, or flash a major credit card, money is behind each transaction.

"Why", you ask, "would she be writing about money management in a parenting book?" Let me tell you why! Many divorces are a result of conflict over money and poor money management. Neither formal money management training nor parenting skills are pre-requisites for adulthood. Experience seems to be the most popular teacher. If parents do a good job teaching children about spending and saving money, most likely, children will be financially responsible adults. But if children are not taught how to wisely manage money, they will likely encounter money management problems in their families which could result in its breakup.

> *If parents do a good job teaching children about spending and saving money, most likely, children will be financially responsible adults.*

MATERIAL GIRLS (AND BOYS)

Children are bombarded by advertisements. Television, billboards, computer screens, DVD's, radios, and movie theaters lure them to want (and think they *need*) everything! Producers of popular kid's movies market promotional products through fast food chains and television commercials. Parents can get a cartoon character watch or stuffed toy with a kid's meal purchase. Entertainment corporations own franchise stores in shopping malls across the country. Adults and kids proudly sport cartoon characters embroidered on expensive clothes. Cyberspace has its own toy stores for purchasing anything from bug boxes to custom computers.

> *Parents must battle children's demands for all the popular gadgets, toys, and entertainment options that invade their senses.*

Material *things* are essential for social acceptance, wealth, and happiness, if you pay attention to social trends today. Television invades our homes with constant commercials, targeting kids to purchase everything from cereal to the latest video game. Products display real kids' pictures on the box. Many television programs don't represent the average family's standard of living. Television families live in nicer homes, wear better clothing, and have more professional and higher salary jobs than the average family who watches TV, therefore encouraging the desire for more material possessions than many parents can afford to buy. Children want the vacation, boat, sports car, latest DVD player, and sports equipment advertised on television. Parents must battle children's demands for all the popular gadgets, toys, and entertainment options that invade their senses. Advertisements encourage children to want and ask for everything!

Talk to children realistically about advertisements. Tell them companies pay for these ads to promote their products and want us to believe their products are best. Teach them to compare products and prices. Ask them to consider if they really *need* it? Give them choices in what you are willing to buy to "test" whether the purchase is a priority for them. Question the claims products make. Help them decide if they really want to break open that piggy bank to buy that special toy.

TEACH A DIFFERENT ATTITUDE

The *attitude* parents have about material things is important in teaching children how to handle money. If owning lots of things is a top priority, then kids will get the idea that material wealth is necessary for success. Likewise, if parents are frugal with spending, kids won't feel the need for as many "things." Richard J. Foster's book, *Celebration of Discipline*,[1] gives a list of ways to express simplicity in life. His principles about spending essentially state that what we buy must have a useful purpose. Seven of Foster's ten principles deal with decisions about material things:

Principle #1:
BUY THINGS FOR THEIR USEFULNESS
INSTEAD OF THEIR STATUS.

A Chevrolet might drive just as well as a BMW. A pair of Lee jeans may wear as well as the Hilfiger brand. Don't purchase things as a status symbol. Teenagers, especially, find this a hard lesson to learn. Teens want the brand names their friends own regardless of price or quality. Parents may have to set spending limits and allow teens to decide how to spend the cash. For example, a teenager may decide that a $60 pair of jeans wasn't such a smart purchase when two pairs of $30 jeans would mean fewer trips to the washing machine. Parents can also offer to split the cost of an item with demanding teens. Let them put their money where their desire is!

When our daughter was a young teenager, she wanted an expensive brand name purse. I offered to pay $40 (a reasonable amount for purchasing a purse) and told her she could come up with the balance if she wanted the more expensive purse. And she did! Splitting the cost of things children want teaches them responsibility for spending. If children aren't willing to spend their money to buy things, it may not be that desirable.

Principle #2:
GET RID OF ANYTHING THAT YOU THINK YOU CAN'T LIVE WITHOUT!

Never let food, electronic gadgets, a hobby, sport, music or ANYTHING control YOU. Get rid of anything that interferes with relationships. People are more important than things.

> *If children aren't willing to spend their money to buy things, it may not be that desirable.*

Our ten-year-old son learned this lesson when neighborhood kids were attracted to playing at our house because of his new video game system. Jonathan became frustrated because kids came to play the video games rather than play outside in the tree house, ride bicycles, or play basketball with him! His frustration led him to sell the entire video game system.

Principle #3:
GIVE IT AWAY!

Choose to give things away—-things you don't use or need. Several years ago, my mother, sister, and I had to clean out my grandmother's two-story home she and my grandfather had lived in for thirty years. She never threw anything away! Because of failing eyesight and diminished mental capacity in her nineties, she couldn't distinguish between junk and valuables. So she kept everything!! We spent four days going through her belongings, discovering both trash and treasures, including an entire closet full of mail order items that had never been used! My mother came home and vowed to start cleaning out her closets so that if something happened to her she would not be embarrassed by clutter!

If you move very often, you learn how much stuff you accumulate. (Look in your attic, drawers, and closets!) While cleaning closets, pantry shelves, and drawers, give away or throw away anything that hasn't been used in the past year. Give away clothes not worn in the last two seasons. Styles change, too. You don't want to be caught with a closet full of unstylish clothes! It takes *too* long for clothes to come back in style to justify keeping them! When my children were young, we always had a garage sale or a giveaway before Christmas to make room for new toys from Santa.

Principle #4:
REFUSE TO ALWAYS BUY WHAT'S HOT IN GADGETS.

New computers, upgraded online services, cell phones with all the latest features, newest style shoes, bread machines, salad makers, coffee grinders, silk fingernails, and the newest model car are "things" we are tempted to purchase. Toss the salad yourself. Paint your own fingernails. Make bread by hand. (Machine made bread is *machine* made bread—not homemade!) Many purchases are prompted by advertisements that appeal to our senses and lead to impulse buying. (The advertisement that talks about coffee being the best part of every morning really makes me want to get up and drink a cup of coffee at daylight until I see the commercial about the pill that guarantees a good night's sleep. Then, I want to go to bed!)

Never, never, never buy on impulse! When shopping, decide in advance a list of purchases and a dollar limit to spend so temptation doesn't lead to impulse buying. "But what if I find a really special dress and it's on sale?" you ask. Don't buy it right then unless you are sure you need it. Ask the store clerk to hold it for a day to give you time to decide if you really want it. Or better yet, wait a week. If you still think you can't live without it, consider purchasing it. Talking to a trusted friend who knows your shopping habits may also reduce spending. Check out garage sales or thrift shops for things you want. Somebody else probably thought he had to have it, too, bought it, and is now getting rid of it!

Principle #5:
DECIDE THAT YOU CAN ENJOY THINGS WITHOUT PURCHASING THEM.

Vacation homes, recreational vehicles, DVDs, boats, and other luxuries can be rented when you need them. Rent a condo for a week's vacation or an RV when you want to take a trip. It will be available to you when you need it but you won't have the clutter or the upkeep. I spent the Fourth of July holiday last year shopping for a new air conditioner and having it installed in the family beach house instead of enjoying the sun and surf! With ten people vacationing for the holiday weekend, we had to be cool, and as owners it was our responsibility to replace or repair! Most people I know who own a recreational vehicle have to build a garage (sometimes as big as their home!) in which to store it!

Principle #6:
CULTIVATE A STRONG APPRECIATION FOR NATURE.

Turn off the television. Take a walk. Watch the squirrels and birds in your backyard. Go to the park. Sit on the beach and watch the sunset—or sunrise if you are an early bird! Find fun entertainment that doesn't cost money. Spending time enjoying nature gives a quiet time to mediate and reflect. When you participate in a nature walk with a loved one, precious moments of communication can be shared.

Principle #7:
AVOID DEBT.

Don't use credit cards for impulse buying. If you can't afford to pay cash, you probably don't need the product (a home and car are generally exceptions). You can save to pay cash for a new car if you save the payment amounts after the car note is paid. (This takes discipline! You may consider having the amount automatically deducted from your checking account each month into savings).

Use a credit card only when you pay the entire balance each month.

Good spending habits are more easily CAUGHT than TAUGHT. When parents have a healthy attitude about material things and their value, chil-

> *Good spending habits are more easily CAUGHT than TAUGHT.*

dren will learn that relationships and responsible money management are more important than owning the newest and most popular "things".

SET THE EXAMPLE IN SPENDING AND SAVING

Teaching children about appropriate spending and saving is an important task for parents. To be effective, parents must have a good plan for managing money. If money management is not your strong point, use this chapter to develop discipline with finances and effective techniques to teach children. Learn to effectively manage money to avoid disagreements in the family.

Setting financial goals for saving and limits for spending are principles that children should learn about money management. Parents must set the example. Remember, instruction to children is *caught* more than *taught*.

Children will likely follow behavior they see and hear. If parents spend lots of money on clothes, children will consider expensive clothing purchases a priority. If parents invest money in stocks and mutual funds, children will learn that savings and investing are important.

What do parents teach children about money? People do two things with money: spend and save. Parents must teach the significance of wise spending *and* saving. Saving money can begin with a piggy bank at home and progress to a bank or brokerage account. Saving includes long-term and short-term goals. Kids can learn to save money to buy a new CD, bicycle, or toy. Long-term goals include saving for college or an automobile when they are old enough to drive.

> *Parents must teach the significance of wise spending and saving.*

Teaching children to spend money *responsibly* can be taught by using a budget. A budget is a short-term spending plan that sets aside income and distributes it for specific uses. A college student I talked with recently uses the "envelope" system for budgeting. (Her dad is a financial planner!) Dad sends a certain dollar amount each month designated for specific living expenses. The cash goes in labeled envelopes for food, telephone, gas, personal items, etc. She uses the cash from each envelope during the month. When the money is gone, the spending stops. As she detailed this budgeting plan with me, she was bursting with pride that she managed to eat on only three dollars the previous week! College students are pros at sniffing out free food and $2.99 burger specials at the local night spots!

Wise money management is a desirable biblical concept. God holds us accountable for the use of money. Jesus tells the story in Luke 19:11-26 about the nobleman who left servants in charge of his money while he was away on a trip. He was pleased with the servant who had wisely invested his money and earned ten times the amount of money that was entrusted to him. The nobleman was angry at the servant who hid his money in the dirt because the money had not earned any interest. God intends for us to use money wisely and productively. Proverbs 11:1 says, "A false balance is an abomination to the Lord, But a just weight is His delight." God is pleased when we act responsibly with money.

Teaching children to spend money responsibly can be taught by using a budget.

CHAPTER 14:

"GIMME, GIMME, GIMME!"

TEACHING YOUNG CHILDREN ABOUT MONEY

When and how do parents teach children about spending money? Moms and dads understand the importance of teaching the value of money when children say, "gimme, gimme, gimme" every time they shop. Around age three, kids begin to make decisions on their own: what kind of drink to order, which toy to purchase, which brand of cereal to buy, etc. Three-year-olds watch television and begin asking for things advertised. They typically don't understand the connection between things they want and the amount of money needed to purchase items, but they have become a consumer force. Think about the popular toys each Christmas that parents are willing to fight over at the stores so that sweet little Susie will have that special toy under the tree on Christmas morning! Adults are reduced to childish behavior—fighting over that doll in the department store because a three-year-old saw the doll that talks, walks, and spits advertised on television and said, "Mommy, I want that!"

In the preschool years, talk to children about the cost of items and set a limit on spending when shopping. For example, one mom says, when she takes a young child to the grocery store, she will agree to buy *one* special treat. The child can choose (within limits) that special treat for himself. The little one knows he will come home with a treat. Parents may choose to give a small child a couple of dollars to purchase an item at the store. Talk about what his money will buy. Let him choose an item and see if he is willing to exchange his cash for the item. This is when spenders and savers are identified!

Teach preschoolers about money by playing money games at home. Using play money, you can play "store" with them to help them grasp the concept of what things cost. When required to "pay" for things and give up dollars, kids will understand the concept of money. During snack time, provide coins for children to purchase snacks. Have them "buy" snacks from the "snack store." A nickel buys a cookie, a dime purchases a glass of chocolate milk, a penny gets a piece of gum, candy, or carrot stick— maybe five carrot sticks to encourage good eating habits!

> *Teach preschoolers about money by playing money games at home.*

Teaching the value of money can also be accomplished by having children practice counting coins from a jar. Teach the value of each coin, e.g., one nickel equals the value of five pennies. Five nickels equal the value of one quarter. Practice this with youngsters. They will learn quickly the worth of coins. (Ponder this: Why is a dime more valuable than a nickel yet it is smaller?)

WHAT ABOUT ALLOWANCES?

By second grade, most children can count money. They recognize coins and know the value of coins and can add and subtract money. When children have grasped the concept of money, parents can begin giving an allowance. A few dollars a week for a child aged six or seven will allow him the freedom and responsibility of spending, giving, and saving. Determine in advance what allowance money is expected to buy. (A personal note, at seven and eight years old, our children were required to pay for special treats and toys. If my children wanted to stop for ice cream or go to the toy store, and I wasn't willing to purchase the items, I suggested they spend their allowances. The children were given the choice to spend or save.) Kids are notorious for a "gimme, gimme" attitude whether they *really* want something or not. When the choice requires them to use their money, children may decide against spending.

School age children can learn to help with shopping and be given choices. Make a game of shopping at the grocery store. Give each child coupons of items to buy. Put them in charge of finding the items in the store and bringing them to the basket. (Letting a child shop in the store alone is only appropriate for older children in today's environment I am sad to confess). Ask them to compare brands and prices and help decide which product is the

> *When the choice requires them to use their money, children may decide against spending.*

best deal. One task that I used in teaching my kids to work together was to allow them to choose *one* cereal or *one* snack between the two of them. When this resulted in an argument, I did not take sides. I simply told them to work together and choose their product before I checked out or we wouldn't buy any. On more than one occasion, they would find me at the checkout counter and come running with their treat like a couple of race horses in the final turn of the Kentucky Derby!

MONEY FOR HOUSEHOLD CHORES?

Whether or not allowances should be tied to chores or achievements is under scrutiny. Advantages to providing children with an allowance for doing certain chores is that it teaches them responsibility for earning money. It provides an incentive for performing certain tasks and rewards them for work. The disadvantages of tying an allowance to chores is that children may think work is not required unless they receive an incentive. Work for pay may also eliminate the desire for work if they aren't motivated by money. Money can also be used as a power play against parents when children don't want to perform a task. Personally, our children received an allowance for specific tasks like retrieving the newspaper and mail, taking out the trash, or emptying the dishwasher. They were not rewarded for taking care of their own toys or room because taking care of their own possessions was their responsibility. That was an expected behavior without extrinsic reward.

MONEY FOR GOOD GRADES?

Should children be given money for good grades? This is a good incentive for some children if they are motivated by money. Others may not respond to cash incentives. By paying for good grades, children may learn that their best effort is not expected without some extrinsic reward. Parents want to teach children to acquire a good education for the intrinsic value. As an alternative to cash, other incentives (a new video game, a special party with friends, or a special item of clothing) may be offered to celebrate achievement.

As an alternative to cash, other incentives may be offered to celebrate achievement.

When our daughter, Melissa, was a junior in high school, we offered her a telephone line if she could achieve all A's for the fall semester. My motivation was to improve her grade point average since she was close to making a decision about college. I knew she wanted the phone line (and I wanted it, too, to get her off my line!). My proposition failed. Melissa did not reach the goal of straight A's which was a greater disappointment to me than to her. (I am not sure if I was disappointed more about the grades or the need for the extra phone line.) I did give her the telephone service anyway as a surprise Christmas present that year because I felt like she worked hard, and I desperately needed a separate phone line. One phone line split between two busy adults, two teenagers, a fax machine and a computer doesn't cut it! The lesson: Make sure the incentive is something

> *Make sure the incentive is something they want and can achieve rather than what parents desire or the plan could backfire!*

they want and can achieve rather than what parents desire or the plan could backfire! My proposal for a personal phone line obviously motivated me more than Melissa!

"MOM, I NEED A RAISE!"

After children have become accustomed to receiving an allowance, they may decide a raise is in order! (Don't we all feel we need a raise?) "Mom, the cost of going to the movies went up!" "My clothes are not in style anymore!" "I really *need* that new CD!" Look at the child's spending habits and decide if they are making responsible decisions with money. Are they saving some portion? Giving some amount to church and charity? Spending the balance in an acceptable manner? If they are showing some responsibility, work out a deal with them to do additional chores for a bonus in their allowance. This will reward their effort and responsible spending, and will give them more chores at home. (That helps parents!)

Age eleven or twelve may be a good time to begin allowing a child to handle money at his own discretion *if he has made good choices with an allowance.* As preteens, my children were given an "entertainment" allowance. *Money was not contingent on doing chores.* An entertainment allowance consisted of a certain dollar amount given on a monthly basis for snacks at school (not lunches—that was my responsibility), DVD rentals, going to the movies or out with friends, or a hamburger at the local fast food restaurant. This allowance was used when *they* wanted something. If parents suggested dinner, movie, or bowling, then we paid for the activity. *But if they desired something more than we were able or willing to give*, the children could use their entertainment allowance for the treat. The allowance provided freedom because I was not constantly saying "no" or "I don't have any money right now." If they wanted to stop at the corner convenience store or fast food restaurant on the way home from school, I could say "yes" because the children had their own money to spend. At first, my children loved the freedom of an entertainment allowance. But, after a few months, they realized the responsibility of managing their own money. They weren't sure it was a "good deal" and quit asking everyday to stop for a treat. (That was a good deal for me!)

> *When children learn to budget money and appreciate special treats, they begin to make better choices with spending.*

GOOD SPENDING HABITS

When children learn to budget money and appreciate special treats, they begin to make better choices with spending. In their book, *Raising Money Smart Kids*,[1] Ron and Judy Blue discuss teaching children how to budget money. Their book teaches using the envelope system, similar to the example of the college student I referred to earlier in the chapter, to show teens how to make spending decisions. Specifically, each envelope is labeled according to the category for spending: saving, tithing, spending, gifts, and clothing. A predetermined amount of money is deposited in each envelope at the beginning of each month. The "Spending" envelope contains cash that can be used for anything they want to purchase. The "Gift" envelope is the amount designated for purchasing Christmas and birthday gifts. Money for clothes is allocated in the "Clothes" envelope. Giving money to church and charities is provided in the "Tithe" envelope. The "Saving" envelope is used for saving money in a bank or brokerage account. The envelope system teaches budgeting skills and the concept of responsible spending.

Like the story shared earlier in this chapter, the envelope system works even for college students. Adults may find it works for their disposable income as well. To determine how much money should be allocated for each spending category, keep up with expenses for a few months and make note of where money is spent. Add together each spending category and allocate money for each.

CHAPTER 15:

TEENAGERS AND MONEY

One divorced mom told me she gave her teenager a portion of her child support check to manage for living expenses (clothes, entertainment, personal care supplies, haircuts, etc.). The teenager knew her mom received a child support check from her dad for her benefit. So mom allowed her the freedom to spend some of the money on personal items. She said, "Susan, this gives my daughter the opportunity to learn responsibility in spending and keeps us from arguing over money. Our relationship is much better when we don't fight over money!"

Monitor the spending habits of teens so that they are spending money for essential items first. What parents consider as essential items (shoes, personal care products) may not be what teens consider essential items (DVD's, jewelry, sports equipment). Keep a written record of what the money is spent for each month. Have the teen keep receipts for purchases.

Teens not only can be responsible for deciding on entertainment and gift purchases but also for buying their own clothes. Try designating a certain amount of money each month for clothes. Allow teens to choose how money is spent each month. If they want an expensive item, encourage *them* to save cash for that special item. Parents will probably want to continue to purchase the necessities such as a winter coat, Sunday outfit, or underwear and socks because teenagers may not consider these items priority! Note: make sure the clothes purchased can be returned, in case they come home with a shirt that doesn't cover enough of the chest or pants that hang too low at the waist!

When children make poor choices in spending, allow them to learn from the experience. Don't rescue them from bad choices. If they purchase a cheap toy or other item that breaks after the first week, empathize with them and talk about how to identify quality products. If parents constantly rescue children from mistakes, they will not learn to be responsible and will depend on mom and dad to bail them out of situations. (I mean literally "bail" them out, too!). Remember, the goal is learning responsible behavior. Children, too, may benefit from making mistakes.

TEENS AND JOBS

Allowances for teens can become a strain on a family's budget. Teens require more money for entertainment, clothes, and gifts. Providing opportunities to work is a good incentive for teaching the rewards of work and reducing the strain on the family budget. Teens learn that part of growing up means providing for their own families. First Timothy 5:8 says, "But if anyone does not provide for his own, and especially for those of his household, he has denied the faith and is worse than an unbeliever." God expects parents to provide for their children and to teach them the responsibility of providing for a family in the future. Our witness as a Christian is reflected in the way we provide for our family and teach children appropriate behavior and values. Teenagers can begin the transition towards self-support with part-time jobs. Jobs help teens to feel confidence in providing for themselves. (As I write this chapter, Roger and I are supporting two college

> *When children make poor choices in spending, allow them to learn from the experience.*

students. *More* money is going out than ever before. I wonder if they will ever be independent. *Say it will happen, Lord!*)

Help teens research job opportunities. Before they can drive or legally hold a job, teens may want to consider jobs such as babysitting, yard work, running errands for neighbors, pet sitting, or other similar tasks. The American Red Cross and other organizations offer babysitting and life-saving courses for specific skills training. Help teens prepare for the job market and be creative in developing job opportunities. For example, teens proficient in the use of computers may offer instructional services to novice computer users. If teens have talent in music, sports, or a specific academic subject, they may offer tutoring services in their area of expertise.

> *Teenagers can begin the transition towards self-support with part-time jobs. Jobs help teens to feel confidence in providing for themselves.*

If parents own a small business, they may take teens to work. By the time my children were ten years old, they worked a few hours a day during summer vacation with their dad at his office. They began by filing papers, emptying trash cans, and cleaning the office. As computer and typing skills became proficient, they could type dictated letters and use the computer system. Roger paid them twice the minimum wage but required them to put half the money in their investment account. (He is an investment representative with a New York Stock Exchange firm—what do you expect!)

Monitor teen employment to insure that a job does not interfere with school achievement. Teens may consider making and spending money more important than an education. A job for a teenager should be a reward for responsible behavior. Make sure they balance work and school. If teens work in high school, parents have the opportunity to monitor this additional responsibility.

CHECKBOOKS AND CREDIT CARDS

The teen years are a good time to teach the responsibility of managing money through a checking account and credit card use. Parents can monitor cash and credit spending and teach young people to balance a checkbook. (Parents must be able to master this task. No, you can't give them the toll-free number to the bank to check balances and outstanding checks!) When my kids graduated from high school, I opened a joint checking account with them at my bank. I monitored their spending and saving habits and helped them balance their accounts at the end of the month. Since our checking accounts were at the same bank, I could monitor their banking habits. (Thanks to personal computer banking, all related accounts are linked and available to monitor on home computers).

They were also allowed to carry *my* credit card (with their name and authorization for use) and use it *with* my approval. They were required to pay me for the charged item when the bill was received. Eventually, *as they demonstrated responsible spending habits*, they were allowed to charge an item without my permission only if they paid me for it when the bill came due.

During the college years, I co-signed a credit card for them to use with the understanding that the balance was paid each month. (I checked this). My teens didn't think this was as much fun as carrying *my* credit card, so they rarely used it. (Lesson learned!)

The reason parents should consider allowing teens to use checks and credit cards is to teach responsibility and monitor usage as a parent. Once teens are out of the home, teaching financial responsibility is much less likely. Many teens who enter the world of work or attend college are bombarded by credit card companies who offer gimmicks to entice teens to apply for credit. Stories of young people who incur thousands of dollars of debt on credit cards with no ability to repay are common knowledge. Without proper parental training in the use of credit cards, teens may become susceptible to poor planning and spending habits that will affect their credit rating. Teaching appropriate credit card use while parents have control is preferable to allowing young adults to make mistakes that affect their credit worthiness. The trend in society towards "cashless" transactions makes the likelihood that people will use credit and debit cards more probable.

> *As parents, our responsibility is to monitor money management as long as we are providing the money.*

REAPING THE REWARDS

As parents, our responsibility is to monitor money management *as long as we are providing the money*. Once parents no longer provide financial support, money management is the adult child's responsibility. This should occur when a child has completed college and/or has begun full-time work. Take your name off credit cards, etc. as the co-signer and allow the child to establish credit in his name. When parents are successful in teaching good spending habits, children will become responsible, independent adults. Parents will be less likely to get that call one day from an adult child asking them to rescue him from a financial crisis.

One experience several years ago gave me confidence that I was doing a good job teaching my children to budget properly. As a 40th birthday gift, Roger, my husband, decided to give me a surprise birthday party at a resort hotel on the bay. He allowed Melissa (she was thirteen at the time) to plan the party within a certain dollar limit. She printed and mailed the invitations, arranged food with the caterer, hired a live band, ordered the cake, and purchased decorations. The hotel coordinator was totally impressed with her abilities to plan and execute this event. (My mom and sister offered their services and were somewhat frustrated that Melissa wanted to do it all herself. Remember the chapter on self-esteem? I don't know why that surprised them. She came into the world doing what she pleased!) Melissa arranged the surprise party and stayed within dad's budget. She was so excited about her achievement, especially since she had just enough money left over after the arrangements were made to purchase a new black dress and shoes for *her* to wear to the party! Years later, she became the social chairman for her college sorority!

CHAPTER 16:

SAVING AND GIVING

Teaching good saving habits is as difficult as teaching appropriate spending habits. Saving money must be a *priority* that we teach our children and teens. A certain amount of money we earn or receive should be set aside for savings. In George S. Clason's *The Richest Man in Babylon*,[1] the Babylonian parable teaches that riches come from understanding the principle that "a part of all you earn is yours to keep." In other words, pay yourself first! Just as a portion of earnings is set aside to pay taxes, give to the church, and pay bills, a portion should also be set aside for saving.

Teaching good saving habits is as difficult as teaching appropriate spending habits.

MOTIVATION TO SAVE

Convincing children to save may require some creativity. Children may not want to save a portion of their allowance, birthday money, or earned income. Parents may have to require saving until children learn the benefits. Set a goal and allow them to save for a new bike, doll, or stereo. *Goal setting* will encourage saving. A *matching plan* may also help children save. Agree to match whatever the child is willing to save, sort of like a matching savings plan at work. The saving incentive is enhanced because the child is actually saving double the amount if parents are willing to match the child's savings. Teach children the Rule of 72. The Rule of 72 tells how long money must be saved at a specified rate in order to double the investment. For example, money earning six percent takes twelve years to double (72 divided by 6 equals 12). Savings that earn nine percent take eight years to double (72 divided by 9 equals 8).

Train little ones to save money by making a game out of depositing change in a piggy bank or a jar. A clear jar allows little ones to see their money that is not being spent. Occasionally, allow them to take money out of the piggy bank for a special toy or treat. Young children think in concrete ways. They can't grasp the idea of saving money by looking at a bank or brokerage statement with numbers on it. They need to see the money with their little eyes.

> As children begin to grasp the concept of money, they can learn different options for saving money.

(Note: parents, beware! College education and weddings cost lots of money. Start saving now! One family told me recently they spent $30,000 on their daughter's wedding. Tuition, room and board at a state university cost about $12,000 annually. On second thought, instead of dropping change in that piggy bank, deposit dollars!)

HOW TO SAVE

As children begin to grasp the concept of money, they can learn different options for saving money. Take them to the bank or brokerage firm and have them open a savings or investment account. To encourage other ways for saving besides bank accounts, talk to children about investing in stocks or stock mutual funds. Children can track prices in the daily newspaper. They can participate in choosing companies for investing money, especially if companies spark an interest such as Disney, Kellogg, Dollar General, and Microsoft. Some companies even provide coupons for shareholders, welcome packets, product samples, and discounts to amusement and theme parks.

Some stock companies offer DRIP plans (dividend reinvestment or direct investment plans) that allow investors to purchase odd lot shares (less than 100 shares) directly from the company. Stock certificates can be issued in the child's name. They will also receive mailings directly from the company. Dividends paid on stock can also be automatically reinvested into more shares for growth.

Mutual funds are often a cheaper way to invest in stocks because they require less money for initial investing and smaller amounts can be added regularly. Investment is distributed among many companies in a mutual fund. Mutual funds, like stocks, provide information to their shareholders about investments. Mutual fund or individual stock investments provide children with incentives and feedback through company mailings and reports periodically.

Collecting is another opportunity for children to save and invest. Baseball cards, coins, and collector dolls are just a few items that children might be interested in collecting. Values can be tracked through books and internet web sites. Trading and selling can be accomplished over the internet, through trade magazines, at flea markets or collector shows. Children learn first hand how an investment can grow and earn more money. Make sure they are keeping track of the cost of their investments.

Parents should begin saving for higher education when a child is born. Setting up a 529 plan will allow money to grow tax exempt as long as the money is used for college expenses. No federal tax deduction is allowed at the time of deposit but earnings are not taxed as they accumulate. If the child chooses not to attend college, the money can be transferred to another person. The account owner controls the distributions for the 529 account.

GIVING MONEY

Learning to give money away is hard for children (and parents!). Children tend to be very selfish not only with possessions but especially with money. Emphasize the importance of "sharing" money by reminding children of their blessings. Explain that many children don't have nice toys, a home, or enough food. Children should recognize the needs of others and learn to help. Giving to church is a top priority. Teach children that God provides everything, and a part of what we have is to be "shared" with God. Children have many opportunities to give: a child at school may have lost his home to a fire, or a friend may have a sick sibling or parent. Parents may choose a specific charity in which the entire family can participate in giving.

Begin teaching young children to give money to church and charities at an early age. Supply giving envelopes for church that can be carried with them. Allow them to put the money in the envelope and *seal* it (so they won't be tempted to take it out before they get to church!). When collectors for various charities come to your door or are encountered at shopping centers, let children hand them money or a check.

Besides teaching kids to give *money* for the good of others, teach them to give their *time*. Volunteering at a soup kitchen, nursing home, women's shelter, Special Olympics, or other charitable organization will help kids to appreciate their personal life situation.

A youth mission trip to inner city Washington, D.C., a few years ago, allowed my teenagers the opportunity to work with underprivileged children. The experience was life-changing for them because they recognized children's desperate need for positive attention, love, and guidance.

One particular little girl became attached to Jonathan, making it hard for him to leave at the end of the week.

This past Christmas, our son, Jonathan, gave his dad a very special Christmas gift. Jonathan had earned 40 dollars raking the yard and planned to buy his dad a gift. Instead, he gave his dad a Christmas card and note explaining that he had given the money to a lady he met during the holidays who was struggling financially. He shared her story in his note and knew his dad would appreciate the money being given to help someone in need. The "gift" was as special to his dad as it was to the lady who received the money.

Training children to be financially responsible is an awesome task. Before it can be taught to children, it must be mastered by parents. Teaching good spending and saving habits now can save parents and children from costly mistakes later!

SUMMARY

Money management is important in family relationships. Teaching good money management to children will help them be successful in future relationships. Poor money management can lead to a failed business or marriage and to tensions in personal relationships because of unpaid debts. Instruction in saving, spending, and giving starts with preschoolers and progresses through childhood and adolescence until parents are no longer financially responsible for children. Parents must model good money management so that children will learn appropriate priorities for spending, saving, and giving.

PART V

SPIRITUAL TRAINING: A PARENT'S MOST IMPORTANT TASK

CHAPTER 17:

WHY IS A FAITH-FILLED LIFE IMPORTANT?

In *Children at Risk* (1990),[1] James Dobson talks about our nation going through a civil war. The chapter titled "The Second Great Civil War" describes two very different and incompatible worldviews battling against each other. The war is a battle for ideas and values. Warriors on one side of the battle are God-fearing people who believe in the Ten Commandments and biblical principles, sanctity of the unborn child, lifelong marriage between a man and a woman, traditional family values, worth of self-discipline, hard work and integrity. Until about 30 years ago, this was the predominant majority view in our country. Generations who lived through two world wars and an economic depression held steadfast to these beliefs.

On the other side of the battlefield, a new way of thinking has emerged. This new society grew out of the "Baby Boom" generation (my generation!) who rebelled against traditional ideals in the 1960s and began to question absolute truths and long-held traditions.

Now, old rules and commandments are being reconsidered. A secular humanistic viewpoint has been embraced, and new priorities have been set. Parental authority has been questioned and weakened by law, giving rights to children to make their own decisions. Early childhood education is required to offer young students a head start, rather than encouraging parental involvement in young children's lives. Classrooms are teaching that gay and lesbian relationships have the same value as heterosexual relationships. Our nation is in a battle today to protect the sanctity of marriage between a man and a woman. Sex education and birth control are provided to students at school which undermines parental authority and values. Social programs broaden the scope of government in our personal lives and burden taxpayers with expanding programs. "Separation of church and state" eliminates religious references in schools and public places. The threat of removing tax-exempt status from nonprofit organizations stifles freedom of speech. The promotion of abortion, euthanasia, and infanticide devalues human life. Women's rights organizations promote agendas that do not emphasize the importance of motherhood. In a secular humanistic viewpoint, there are no moral absolutes.

NEW MORALITY

Over the past 30 years, the "new morality" has taken power in all aspects of society that affect our families. Entertainment through movies, television, music, and books promote violence, sex, and immoral lifestyles. Public education systems have eliminated values education and religious material. Recent studies cite that university professors for the most part are more liberal than the majority of the country's population. Psychological trends try to lessen parental rights and promote rights of the child above respect for authority. Endowments to the arts, including offensive art funded by taxpayers, provide art to the public that is offensive to a moral society. Businesses are burdened by affirmative action programs that promote alternative lifestyles and unfair hiring practices. Scientific research devalues human life by promoting abortion, infanticide and euthanasia. Parental rights are being ignored concerning the health of children. Liberal political organizations are promoting the gay rights agenda, over-taxation of families, and increase in social welfare programs.

Parental rights are being stripped and replaced by government mandates and so-called "rights of the child." In schools, children are taught to accept alternative lifestyles as equal to their own and learn how to practice "safe" sex.

Who is left to fight for the values that parents desire for children? The church and the family. The winner in this war is not yet determined. Traditional churches do not appear to be attracting new converts, even though the desire among young people for spiritual relationships is acknowledged and increasing. Traditional two-parent families in society (Christian and non-Christian) are experiencing a divorce rate at around fifty percent. Less than twenty-five percent of our children grow up in "traditional" family homes consisting of two parents with a stay-at-home mom (according to recent statistics). Children are caught in the middle of this battle—a battle for control of their hearts and minds.

> *The less influence parents exert over children, the more society influences them.*

The less influence parents exert over children, the more society influences them. Society is focused toward this "new morality." Parents must provide children with the *armor* to fight this "civil war of values" as Dr. Dobson calls it. Their minds and spirits are the battlefield for this second great civil war. Those who control what children think and experience will determine the future direction for this country. Will we win this war? Parents will win only if they teach children values and bring them to recognize their need for a relationship with God. The values of an entire generation are at stake.

A strong faith is important for children today. Leading children to a personal relationship with Jesus Christ is parents' most important task. The decision to accept Jesus as Savior belongs to the child, but parents are responsible for teaching about Christ and living a life that will draw children to desire a personal relationship with Him.

Before we can expect children to develop a desire to follow Christ, they must see Christ reflected in the lives of parents. Ask yourself, "Do I have a personal relationship with God? Have I repented of sin and accepted Christ as Lord and Savior?" Most will readily say, "Yes, Jesus is my Savior. I know He died on the cross for my sin and has forgiven me." If your answer is no, consider your need for a personal relationship with Christ.

A harder question is whether He is *Lord* of your life, *Lord* of your marriage, *Lord* of your parenting, *Lord* of your work, *Lord* of your play, *Lord* of your thoughts and *Lord* of your actions. Parents are not perfect but must strive for perfection. Parenting is a difficult task. We need wisdom and strength that can only come from God to be successful and develop a lifelong rewarding relationship with our children.

CHAPTER 18:

HOW TO INFLUENCE SPIRITUAL DEVELOPMENT

Providing a home environment centered on God is the responsibility of parents. Unconditional love is given and provides an environment for children to grow and mature. Faith in God forms a solid foundation from which all attitudes, values, and habits are built.

Studies have been published that research characteristics of successful families. Researchers, including educators, physicians, psychologists, and those from nonprofit organizations and governmental agencies, have conducted studies on family success. Many of these studies contain common threads of traits that make families successful:

1. Respect for each other. Parents treat children with dignity and respect. They say "please" and "thank you" to each other. Children learn to respect parents and others because this behavior is modeled by parents.

2. Family members communicate effectively. Parents listen to children and have the ability to say to the

child, "this is what I hear you saying..." They empathize and connect emotionally with children.

3. Clear parental guidelines are understood concerning right and wrong. Children know what is expected. Discipline is fair.

4. Conflict is resolved in an appropriate manner. Successful families have mastered the art of conflict resolution.

5. Spending time together is a priority. Families set aside time to communicate, encourage, and enjoy each other.

6. A common religious faith is experienced. The opportunity is given for children to learn about faith and participate as a family unit.

Each of the first five characteristics have been discussed in previous sections of this book. Therefore, my purpose here is to develop ideas on growing a spiritual faith in our children.

How do we teach a strong commitment to faith? Parents must *walk* the *talk*. You know what I mean if you have ever heard ugly words from your child's mouth that he first heard come from your mouth! Or you witness a fit of anger from a child that mimics your behavior! Children must see a commitment in our personal lives. In Deuteronomy 6:6-9 we read:

> And these words which I command you today shall be in your heart; you shall teach them diligently to your children, and shall talk of them when you sit in your house, when you walk by the way, when you lie down, and when you rise up. You shall bind them as a sign on your hand, and they shall be as frontlets

between your eyes. You shall write them on the doorposts of your house and on your gates.

That pretty well covers every aspect of life! What a big responsibility! This kind of lifestyle provides a climate in which God can work with children. Remember, faith will be caught more than taught.

PRAYER: TEACHING CHILDREN TO TALK TO GOD

Lead children to a relationship with Christ by teaching them to pray. Begin teaching young children a simple meal-time prayer to thank God for the food He has provided: "God is great. God is good. Let us thank Him for our food. Amen." As children mature, encourage expression in their own words. Pray with children during stressful times (a sick family member, a child studying for a big test the next day at school, or a child auditioning for a role in the school play).

Pray with children in good times. Thank Him for a safe trip at the end of a journey. Thank Him for keeping Mom or Dad safe on the job. Thank Him for the bonus received at work that will pay for the new computer. Thank Him for the beautiful weather or a fun day at the beach.

Pray *with* your children at bedtime. This is the perfect time to encourage a calm, peaceful, and prayerful attitude. Encourage self-expression in prayer. Assure children that God hears and answers prayers. My son as a child would pray for loved ones who had gone to heaven (grandparents and even his dog). Every night, he would name each of the deceased and say, "I hope they like it up there with you, God."

Children need to hear us pray for their individual needs. Two books that give specific words, thoughts, and Scriptures to use in prayer are: *The Power of a Praying Parent* by Stormie O'Martian and *Praying the Bible for Your Children* by David and Heather Kopp. These books provide specific prayers, Bible verses, and topics for which to pray.

A powerful way to pray for children is to kneel beside their beds, after they are asleep, lay your hand on them, and pray. This can be especially calming when children have had a difficult day. The following day parents may witness a peaceful look or calm behavior as a result of diligent prayer.

Pray *anytime, anywhere.* Pray in the car while driving. (Don't close your eyes!) Pray while washing children's clothes. Pray for each child as you fold or iron his clothes. Pray while cooking dinner. Pray while sitting at the ball park on endless summer evenings. Ask God to bring to mind each child's specific needs. Lamentations 2:19 tells us to "pour out your heart like water before the face of the Lord. Lift your hands toward Him for the life of your young children."

"THE B-I-B-L-E: YES, THAT'S THE BOOK FOR ME!"

Read the Bible to children to spark interest. Show them Hebrews 4:12 that says God's word is "living and powerful, and sharper than any two-edged sword, piercing even to the division of soul and spirit, and of joints and marrow, and is a discerner of the thoughts and intents of the heart." Emphasize that God's Word is a place to find answers to life's problems, encouragement for difficult times, assurance of God's love, and guidelines for living. Bedtime may be a good time for Bible reading. Use special devotion books with stories and related Bible verses, songs, and prayers. Read a story each night and discuss it before praying together and saying goodnight. Children love stories. They relate to stories and can identify with characters. Jonathan, as a youngster, loved to see his name in Scripture and hear the Old Testament story of Jonathan and David. Jesus used stories (parables) in His ministry because people could relate easily. Parents can also present the gospel and life of Christ through stories children will enjoy.

OBEDIENCE

Teach Scripture that emphasizes obedience to God and parents. James 1:22 says, "But be doers of the word, and not hearers only." Parents must obey God if children are to learn obedience. (Remember, values are caught more than taught!) God commands children to obey parents. Show children the verse in Colossians 3:20 that says, "Children, obey your parents in all things, for this is well pleasing to the Lord." (When they are teenagers, you may want to share Ephesians 6:2-3 with them that says, *"Honor your father and mother,* which is the first commandment with promise: *that it may be well with you and you may live long on the earth."* Parents may get the urge to physically harm disobedient teenagers...so warn them with Scripture! Just kidding!) When children learn obedience to parents, they can understand what it means to be obedient to God. When we are faithful to God's Word, he blesses us and gives us a deep love and trust in Him. Through His Holy Spirit we are empowered with wisdom.

WISDOM

The Book of Proverbs is filled with principles for living. Introduce children to this Old Testament book that will provide lessons for wise living. Wisdom is the theme of Proverbs and a virtue that children should be taught to desire. Proverbs 2:1-6 says:

> My son, if you receive my words,
> And treasure my commands within you,
> So that you incline your ear to wisdom,
> And apply your heart to understanding;
> Yes, if you cry out for discernment,
> And lift up your voice for understanding,
> If you seek her as silver,
> And search for her as for hidden treasures;
> Then you will understand the fear of the Lord,

And find the knowledge of God.
For the Lord gives wisdom;
From His mouth comes knowledge and
understanding.

BATTLING EVIL

Scripture provides a means to teach children *how* to live a successful life. It tells how to avoid sin and temptation by preparing our hearts and minds for spiritual warfare. Ephesians 6:10-18 says:

> Finally, my brethren, be strong in the Lord and in the power of his might. Put on the whole armor of God, that you may be able to stand against the wiles of the devil. For we do not wrestle against flesh and blood, but against principalities, against powers, against the rulers of the darkness of this age, against spiritual hosts of wickedness in the heavenly places. Therefore take up the whole armor of God, that you may be able to withstand in the evil day, and having done all, to stand. Stand therefore, having girded your waist with truth, having put on the breastplate of righteousness, and having shod your feet with the preparation of the gospel of peace; above all, taking the shield of faith with which you will be able to quench all the fiery darts of the wicked one. And take the helmet of salvation, and the sword of the Spirit, which is the word of God; praying always with all prayer and supplication in the Spirit, being watchful to this end for all perseverance and supplication for all the saints...

Children need to know how to battle evil and depend on guidance from God's holy Scripture. Because evil is not always recognized, children must be aware of what constitutes "good" and "evil". Strong moral judgment is the best defense against evil.

REVERENCE

Teach obedience and a reverence for God through Scripture. Proverbs 1:7 says, "The fear of the Lord is the beginning of knowledge." Fearing God means to reverence Him, desire to please Him, fear his displeasure. Children need to know God is a fair and just God. He disciplines those He loves. Revelation 3:19: "As many as I love, I rebuke and chasten. Therefore be zealous and repent." Children learn about God's discipline when parents discipline them. When parents are fair and just with discipline, children will believe God is fair and just, too. When children become young adults, they will be equipped to obey God because they have obeyed parents. Instill in them a reverence for God and a desire to please Him.

> *Strong moral judgment is the best defense against evil.*

MUSIC FOR LITTLE HEARTS

Children love to sing! Scripture is easily memorized when set to music. My guess is that if you were raised in church, you could sing a song right now that is a Scripture verse! Consider teaching little ones praise and worship choruses based on Scripture. Songs played and sung while driving in the car or at bedtime can produce a calming spirit in children (and parents!)

Remember the battle for the hearts and minds of children mentioned at the beginning of this section? Children's minds must be filled with God's Word so that they are empowered for the spiritual warfare ahead!

GUARD YOUR HEART

Teach children to guard their hearts and minds. Proverbs 4:23 says, "Keep your heart with all diligence, for out of it spring the issues of life." In Philippians 4:6-7 Paul writes to the church at Philippi, "Be anxious for nothing, but in everything by prayer and supplication, with thanksgiving, let your requests be made known to God; and the peace of God, which surpasses all understanding, will guard your hearts and minds through Christ Jesus."

The peace of God will guard our hearts and minds when we pray. Jeremiah 29:11 says that God has wonderful plans for life: "For I know the thoughts that I think toward you, says the Lord, thoughts of peace and not of evil, to give you a future and a hope."

Children need to learn to guard their hearts and minds against sin. One little girl asked her mom, "Mommy, is it a sin if you don't see me?" The mother replied, "God always sees you." God equips us with the ability to resist sin when we focus on His Word.

> *What is allowed in our minds through seeing and hearing is what will come out as talk and attitudes.*

When teaching teenagers and older children, I discuss the concept of "Garbage In, Garbage Out." What is allowed in our minds through seeing and hearing is what will come out as talk and attitudes. For example, if one plays violent video games, watches sexually explicit movies, hangs around people whose behavior and language is offensive, these things will affect thoughts and actions! This is an important lesson for teenagers who can make devastating mistakes. Proverbs 23:7 tells us, "For as he thinks in his heart, so is he."

POSITIVE ROLE MODELS

Provide children with positive things in their environment. Provide stories, books, and movies that entertain appropriately and teach values. Laura Ingalls Wilder, L. Montgomery, C. S. Lewis, Frank Peretti, Disney, *Feature Films for Families, Adventures in Odyssey,* and *McGee &*

Me are all examples of positive instructional entertainment.

Introduce them to contemporary Christian music: Steven Curtis Chapman, D. C. Talk, Newsboys, Michael W. Smith, Point of Grace, and numerous others who can be heard on Christian radio stations and Christian music cable channels. These Christian artists may sound like rock 'n' roll singers, but their message is from God's Word, and children and teens will embrace it! Christian music can become an alternative to rock music for teens.

Christian summer camps offer intensive Bible study and positive role models. Involve children in church activities. Church offers positive experiences and desirable peer relationships. Parental involvement with teen activities also gives opportunities for parents to have a connection with their teenager's friends.

> *To empower children for wise living, teach them to choose friends and acquaintances wisely.*

FRIENDS—MORE THAN A TELEVISION SHOW

To empower children for wise living, teach them to choose friends and acquaintances wisely. The older they become, the more powerful the influence of friends. Get involved in helping them choose good friends. How can this be accomplished? When children are young, look ahead to activities in which your children could be involved at school and church and start steering them in the direction of positive peer groups. For example, does the middle and high school have a strong band program? Is this where bright and popular kids participate? Is a particular sports program exceptional in a community? What church provides a growing children's and youth ministry? What community-based programs are reaching children and teens in your area?

Talk to children about qualities to look for in friends. Proverbs 13:20 says, "He who walks with wise men will be wise, but the companion of fools will be destroyed." Talk about looking for characteristics of honesty, integrity, trustworthiness, a disciplined lifestyle, compassion, and generosity. Discuss why these are desirable traits in choosing close friends. Good friends will encourage appropriate behaviors and success. Talk about why they should avoid bad friends who will lead them astray. Remind them that the Bible says beware of bad company: "My son, if sinners entice you, do not consent" (Pr 1:10). "Do not be deceived: 'Evil company corrupts good habits'" (1 Co 15:33). Teach that friends who encourage wrongdoing are selfish and should be avoided.

> *Self-discipline in children is key in avoiding many temptations that lurk in preteen and teen years.*

My son has been blessed with a close group of friends who have been together since third grade. They share church and high school memories. Although they have gone to separate (rival!) universities, they still get together during holidays and summer breaks. The closeness they shared in their growing up years will be a lifelong treasure for them.

SELF-DISCIPLINE

Self-discipline in children is key in avoiding many temptations that lurk in preteen and teen years. Encourage good nutrition, adequate sleep, physical exercise, and discipline in practicing music, sports and schoolwork. Self-discipline in personal care will yield confidence in children to say "no" to drugs, alcohol, and sexual desires when faced with temptation.

Talk to children about these temptations by age ten or eleven. The influences of drugs, sex, and alcohol are becoming more prevalent by fifth and sixth grades. Many children are exposed to drug and alcohol use and sexual experimentation *before* middle-school years. Childhood is limited for children because of evil influences of society through media and the breakdown of families. Role play with children answers that will provide a way to say "no."

"I really don't like the taste of beer."

"Smoking gives me a bad taste in my mouth."

"I can have fun without taking pills."

Postpone socializing with the opposite sex as long as possible. Girls generally mature much faster than boys and are interested in boys *before* boys are interested in them! Minimize boy/girl activities in early teen years. Interest in the opposite gender will come soon enough.

Eating disorders such as anorexia nervosa and bulimia are prevalent today among teenage girls. These are dangerous and life-threatening diseases that require medical and psychological treatment. Teenage girls are determined to literally starve themselves to death because of a fallacy in thinking they are overweight, in addition to other psychological problems. Emphasize good nutrition and keep communication open with teenage girls to avoid the plague of eating disorders.

> *Temptation can be pleasurable, so don't play around with it.*

Apostle Paul tells Timothy in 2 Timothy 2:22 to "flee youthful lusts." Teach teens to avoid situations that will tempt them sexually. The command "to flee" shows the danger of youthful temptations. Paul doesn't say just turn away but rather turn and run in the opposite direction. *Flee!* Temptation can be pleasurable, so don't play around with it. Emphasize dangers of sexual experimentation to preteens. When they learn to discipline their own bodies, parents can feel more confident in their kids' ability to avoid dangerous behaviors such as sex, drugs, alcohol, smoking, and eating disorders.

TALK THE RIGHT TALK!

"Watch what you say," moms command. Children today are exposed to profanity and inappropriate language through media, friends, school, and other social venues in which they are involved, not to mention their own homes. It is critical to teach (and model) appropriate and positive speech to children.

The "Garbage in, Garbage Out" concept applies not only to thoughts but also to speech. Garbage in from what is *heard* means garbage out of the *mouth* through what we say. Proverbs 4:24 says, "Put away from you a deceitful mouth, and put perverse lips far from you." One mother told me that her four-year-old daughter thought the family cat's name was "darn cat" because that's the only name she heard her daddy call the cat!

Emphasize the importance of always speaking the truth and encouraging others with words.

Colossians 4:6 tells us how we *should* speak. "Let your speech always be with grace, seasoned with salt, that you may know how you ought to answer each one." Emphasize the importance of always speaking the truth and encouraging others with words. Speech should build up and not put down. Gossip, negative criticism, and foul language are not constructive speech. "Garbage in. Garbage out." Don't ponder bad thoughts that will result in negative and destructive talk.

The Book of Proverbs is full of verses that emphasize importance of speech:

10:11: "The mouth of the righteous is a well of life, but violence covers the mouth of the wicked."

10:20: "The tongue of the righteous is choice silver; the heart of the wicked is worth little."

10:21: "The lips of the righteous feed many, but fools die for lack of wisdom."

10:32: "The lips of the righteous know what is acceptable, but the mouth of the wicked what is perverse."

12:18: "There is one who speaks like the piercings of a sword, but the tongue of the wise promotes health."

12:22: "Lying lips are an abomination to the Lord, but those who deal truthfully are His delight."

Teach children that God desires to give wisdom, knowledge and power for daily living.

15:7: "The lips of the wise disperse knowledge, but the heart of the fool does not do so."

20:15: "There is gold and a multitude of rubies but the lips of knowledge are a precious jewel."

12:22: "Lying lips are an abomination to the Lord, but those who deal truthfully are His delight."

A DESIRE FOR THE FRUIT OF THE SPIRIT

Galatians 5:22-23 says, "But the fruit of the Spirit is love, joy, peace, longsuffering, kindness, goodness, faithfulness, gentleness, self-control. Against such there is no law." Teach children attitudes and behaviors that are pleasing to God. When Jesus lives in hearts through the indwelling of the Holy Spirit, one can experience the fruit of the Spirit.

God gives us *power* in our lives to be obedient to His commands because He gives the power of the resurrection.

Teach children that God desires to give wisdom, knowledge and power for daily living (2 Ti 1:7). Then, model the
power God gives in your own life.

Ephesians 1:17-20 tells us:

> That the God of our Lord Jesus Christ, the Father of
> glory, may give to you the spirit of wisdom and reve-
> lation in the knowledge of Him, the eyes of your
> understanding being enlightened; that you may
> know what is the hope of His calling, what are the
> riches of the glory of His inheritance in the saints,
> and what is the exceeding greatness of His power
> toward us who believe, according to the working of
> His mighty power which he worked in Christ when
> He raised Him from the dead and seated Him at His
> right hand in the heavenly places. . . . "

Philippians 3:10-11 talks about the depth of desire to
know Christ. Paul says "that I may know Him and the power
of His resurrection, and the fellowship of His sufferings, being
conformed to His death, if, by any means, I may attain to the
resurrection from the dead." Children should be taught to
desire a deep personal relationship with Christ to receive
power He gives for successful living. 2 Timothy 1:7 says, "for
God has not given us a spirit of fear, but of power, and of love,
and of a sound mind."

Through Scripture children can be are encouraged and
reminded that God empowers His people to live an abundant
life and desires that for us. Jesus said in John 10:10, "I have
come that they may have life, and that they may have it
more abundantly." Promises in Scripture produce a *desire* to
be obedient to God because of the blessings He delivers.

HOW CHILDREN SEE GOD

Influencing how a child sees God is a challenge. They picture Him in their little minds as a person and don't have the

capacity to think in abstract ways. So questions like "Does God get a cold?" are perfectly normal and delightful. A child's view of God is largely influenced by the love and support from family. His perception of God will depend on how well the family relates to him the depth of a personal relationship to God. If parents show children unconditional love, affection, availability to their needs, grace and mercy, and fair and just discipline, they will see God as loving, just, gracious, merciful, and available. If children live in a home filled with neglect, conditional love, vindictiveness, unreasonable demands, unfair punishment, and absence of love, they will perceive God as unreasonable, unloving, harsh, unjust, and vengeful. To develop a healthy image of God, children need a loving and trustworthy relationship with parents. Therefore, it is important that parents model God's character so children develop a healthy image of God. The image of God that parents cultivate in children will greatly determine a child's desire for a personal relationship with Him.

> *A child's view of God is largely influenced by the love and support from family.*
>
> *To develop a healthy image of God, children need a loving and trustworthy relationship with parents.*

Children see God through parents' behaviors. Be open and honest. Create an environment at home where children can express feelings—even anger, frustration, and disappointment. Teach them to express emotions appropriately. Listen to their needs. Teach forgiveness and ask forgiveness. Show unconditional love and value. Children need to know that God values them and made them special. Fair and consistent discipline teaches a child that God is a just God and can be trusted to lead them. Teaching by example encourages children to live a Christ-like life.

CHAPTER 19

PUTTING IT ALL TOGETHER

Teaching these specific attributes and attitudes about God is the most important task to prepare children for developing a personal relationship with God through Jesus Christ. Like most behavior children learn from parents, a desire for a personal relationship with Christ will be *caught* more than *taught*. That places a tremendous responsibility on parents!

Try every day to model desired behaviors. Children need to hear parents pray for and with them, read and study the Scripture, talk about what God expects in our lives, share God's love and truth with others, speak with a pure heart, and encourage others through words and deeds. They need to *see* a consistent Christian life through behavior and attitudes: giving to the church, being responsible for finances, showing compassion to others, doing good deeds for the less fortunate and loving each other. Parents must *walk the walk*, not just talk the talk! Parents are the most significant influence in a child's life. Our actions speak louder than words.

> *Parents are the most significant influence in a child's life.*

One of my dad's favorite sayings was "Do as I say, not as I do." (He said that because he was a smoker and did not want his children to smoke!) However, in parenting, that saying doesn't work very well. Values are more easily caught than taught! Children will most likely do what parents do. Parents must set the example.

Teachable Moments. Look for teachable moments with children. Life experiences provide life lessons from which children can relate. When a favorite pet dies, teach children that God is a loving God and He cares about hurt and pain. Tell them that explanations can't always be found for why things happen. When China, our family's Labrador retriever, died, our five-year-old son grieved over the loss of his buddy. He sat and cried over the dog's grave. Eventually, he began to realize that he could not go to heaven with China and prayed that God would take care of her in heaven. (After some time, we got a new family dog which he grew to love).

On another occasion, I witnessed my child tell the store clerk that he had been undercharged for a purchase. The store clerk was amazed and complimented him for his honesty. I used the opportunity to affirm his honesty and remind him that such actions pleased God.

When my ninety-three-year-old grandmother came to live with our family several years ago while recovering from a broken leg, my children amazed me with their care, compassion, and willingness to accept additional responsibility. They loved wheeling her around the house in her wheelchair and playing with her wheelchair when she was in bed. They played games with her and served her meals. (They left the bedpan job to me, however!) Life experiences become teachable moments for children to learn about God's character.

LIVING THE SPIRIT-FILLED LIFE

Josh McDowell, noted youth culture specialist, wrote *The Disconnected Generation,*[1] in which he talks about a missing connection in relationships with today's youth. He named six keys to communicating effectively with youth to gain connectedness: affection, acceptance, affirmation, appreciation, availability, and accountability. Children must connect with parents and other significant adults in their lives and be convinced of their spiritual relationship before children can believe it themselves. Parents should model the Christian life, teach God's truth, and seize teachable moments along the way. Then, leave the rest to God and pray that children are convinced in their own hearts and minds of the awesome love of God and their need for Him.

Modeling a consistent Christian lifestyle gives parents confidence that children will possess a good image of God and desire a personal relationship with Him. Trust God to draw children to Himself after they have been given the foundation for spiritual development through a healthy family life. Children are gifts from God whom He has entrusted to parents. The responsibility belongs to moms and dads to teach children about His character. God will bless our commitment of teaching and living a consistent Christian life. Children will make mistakes, and not all children will follow the desired path. But equipping children with tools for living will minimize the likelihood for costly mistakes.

John Ashcroft, United States Attorney General and professed Christian, wrote a book about his father's influence in his life, *Lessons from a Father to His Son*.[2] The book is bursting with stories and lessons his father taught him about living his faith and is a great example of the consistent

> *Modeling a consistent Christian lifestyle gives parents confidence that children will possess a good image of God and desire a personal relationship with Him.*

Christian lifestyle being "caught" by a child. A very touching story was told about the day Ashcroft was sworn into the United States Senate in 1995. This is Ashcroft's story:

> The night before I was sworn in to the Senate in 1995, my father arranged for some close friends and family—maybe fifteen or twenty people—to gather for dinner. My father eyed a piano in the corner of the room and said, 'John, why don't you play the piano and we'll sing?' Okay, dad. You name it, I'll play it. . . . After the song, I eased away from the piano keys and found myself thinking out loud. 'We're standing here having a good time,' I said, 'but I really wish we were in a dedication service. . . . ' My lifelong friend, Dick Foth, spoke up, 'We can do something about a dedication service, John.' At Dick's suggestion, we gathered early the next morning at a house not far from the Capitol. . . . We began by chatting informally and then sang a hymn or two. At the time I did not realize how weak my father was, but he had been losing weight through the months of November and December and had told an acquaintance of his, 'I'm hanging on by a thread, and it's a thin thread at that, but I'm going to see John sworn into the Senate.' As we talked, the earnestness of my father's voice suddenly commanded everyone's attention. 'John,' Dad said, 'please listen carefully.' My children and I fixed our focus on Dad. . . .' The spirit of Washington is arrogance,' my dad said, 'and the spirit of Christ is humility. Put on the spirit of Christ. Nothing of lasting value has ever been accomplished in arrogance.' The room was absolutely quiet. . . . 'Someday I hope that someone will come up to you as you're fulfilling your duties as a senator, tug on your sleeve, and say 'Senator, your spirit

is showing.'. . After we discussed my father's words, I finally asked that we have a time of solemn prayer. . . . I knelt in front of the sofa where my father was seated, and everyone gathered around me. Most placed a hand on my head, shoulders, or back. Everyone was standing when I noticed my father lunging, swinging his arms, trying to lift himself out of the couch, one of those all-enveloping pieces of furniture that tends to bury you once you sit in it. Given my father's weakness—a damaged heart operating at less than one-third capacity—getting out of that couch was taking a major-league effort. Dad was not making much progress. I felt terrible. Knowing he did not have strength to spare, I said, 'Dad, you don't have to struggle to stand and pray over me with these friends.' 'John,' my father answered, 'I'm not struggling to stand, I'm struggling to kneel' . . . He was not struggling to stand, he was struggling to kneel. I was taken back to those early mornings half a century before when I slipped underneath my father and joined him on his knees. He prayed then that we would do noble things. Now, still on his knees, he was taking me there. I was overwhelmed, humbled, and inspired all at once. . . . Some fathers deal with their sons eyeball to eyeball; others, nose-to-nose. In the end, my father dealt with me knee-to-knee.

Ashcroft's father died later that night after witnessing his son's induction into the United States Senate. Ashcroft's book is a testament of a father's legacy that was both "taught" and "caught" and inspired a son to do great things. This is every parent's goal. When a relationship with Christ becomes real to children, then God is honored. He will bless obedience to Him through the impression made on children.

Parents can reap the rewards of spiritual training of children throughout their lifetime as they watch children grow in love and obedience to God.

SUMMARY

The materialistic, secular society of today's culture is not conducive to spiritual training of children. Teaching children about God and how He desires for us to live must come from the home. Successful relationships in life are correlated with a strong commitment to faith. Parents are responsible for teaching children about God's character, prayer, Scripture reading, and the necessity of guarding their hearts and minds, and modeling a Christ-like lifestyle. When our relationship with God becomes real to children, they will desire a personal relationship with Him, and God will be honored.

> *Parents can reap the rewards of spiritual training of children throughout their lifetime as they watch children grow in love and obedience to God.*

RAISING GREAT KIDS IN A TOUGH WORLD

My great-niece turned one year old yesterday. As I watched her toddle around on those chubby little feet with mom and dad opening her birthday presents, I realized for them that the parenting journey is just beginning. Raising children is an awesome task. As I look back on the journey, I sometimes ask, "How did we do it?" Life is busy and full of challenges during the growing-up years. I miss those days of hugs, kisses, and adoration. Soccer games, piano recitals, choral concerts, proms, movie nights, and birthday parties are all gone. But my heart swells with joy as I watch my two children who have flown from the nest begin to weave their own nests and take their places in the world.

Parenting does not come with instructions as I noted at the beginning of this book. Therefore, the purpose of this book is to provide parents with a guide to help through the journey. Parenting is a challenge because no two children are alike and no two parents always agree. Children encounter different struggles, possess different personalities and talents that must be individually molded. Parenting is a challenge and requires investing time and effort into family life. It is worth the effort and can be a time of satisfaction, joy, and memory building.

This book offers practical advice to parents to guide you through the journey of parenting. Most principles are based on my own research and practical experiences. I share intimate stories of my family's journey to encourage you, knowing that no family is perfect and many face the same challenges you encounter. My purpose is to encourage parents and offer practical advice in five major areas of parenting: building self-esteem, communication, discipline, money matters, and spiritual development.

The bigger picture in parenting involves launching functional healthy children into society where they contribute to the world in a positive way. They become our heritage in life. This is our contribution to the world as effective and loving parents. Parenting is a great, awesome and attainable task. Accept the challenge and enjoy the rewards. You can raise great kids in a tough world.

NOTES

Chapter 1: The Importance of Self-Esteem

1. Anne Ortlund, *Children Are Wet Cement.* (Fleming H. Revell Co., 1981).

Chapter 2: Building Self-Esteem by Actions

1. William Barclay, *Letters to the Galatians and Ephesians* (Westminster John Knox Press, 1976)

2. Gary Chapman & Ross Campbell, *The Five Love Languages of Children.* (Moody Press, 1997).

Chapter 3: Building Self-Esteem by Words and Listening

1. Anne Ortlund, *Children Are Wet Cement.* (Fleming H. Revell Co., 1981).

2. From *The Language Of Love* by Gary Smalley and John Trent, Ph.D., a Focus on the Family book published by Tyndale House. Copyright © 1988, 1991, by Gary Smalley and John Trent, Ph.D. All rights reserved. International Copyright secured. Used by Permission.

3. Franklin Graham, quoted from Focus on the Family taped broadcast, *Rebellious Teenagers.* (Focus On The Family, 1986).

4. Gary Smalley & John Trent, *The Blessing.* (Thomas Nelson, Inc., 1986).

Chapter 4: Positive Communication

1. As quoted by Darrell Scott in *Rachel's Tears*, by Beth Nimmo & Darrell Scott. (Thomas Nelson Publishers, 2000). p. 62-64.

Chapter 5: Yakety-Yak: How We Talk to Kids

1. H. Norman Wright. *The Power Of A Parent's Words.* (Gospel Light/Regal Books, Ventura, CA 93003, 1991). Used by permission.

Chapter 7: Speak Another Language

1. From *The Language Of Love* by Gary Smalley and John Trent, Ph.D., a Focus on the Family book published by Tyndale House. Copyright © 1988, 1991, by Gary Smalley and John Trent, Ph.D. All rights reserved. International Copyright secured. Used by Permission.

2. Gary Chapman & Ross Campbell, *The Five Love Languages of Children.* (Moody Press, 1997).

Chapter 8: Are You Listening?

1. As quoted by Darrell Scott in *Rachel's Tears*, by Beth Nimmo & Darrell Scott. (Thomas Nelson Publishers, 2000). p. 62-64.

Chapter 9: Making Kids Mind Is Good for Kids, Too!

1. Charles R. Swindoll, Christian Family Living Tape Series, *Shaping The Will With Wisdom*. (Insight For Living, 1982). Taken from *Promises to Peter* by Charlie Shedd (W Publishing, 1970).

2. James Dobson, *The Strong Willed Child*. (Tyndale House Publishing, 1978).

Chapter 10: Why Is Discipline Necessary?

1. From *Focus on the Family* magazine Growing Years Edition, Vol.25, No. 5, May 2001, published by Focus on the Family. Copyright © 2001 Focus on the Family. All rights reserved. International copyright secured. Used with permission.

2. Don Dinkmeyer and Gary D. McKay, *Step-Systematic Training For Effective Parenting: The Parent's Handbook*. (American Guidance Service, 1982).

Chapter 12: Results of Effective Discipline

1. As quoted by Misty Bernall & Brad Bernall in *The Turning Point For Cassie Bernall*, by Steven James in Lifeway Magazine, April 2000. Used by permission.

Chapter 13: Money Matters!

1. Richard J. Foster, *Celebration of Discipline*, (Harper and Row Publishers, 1978).

Chapter 14: "Gimme! Gimme! Gimme!"

1. Ron and Judy Blue, *Raising Money Smart Kids*. (Thomas Nelson Publishers, 1992).

Chapter 16: Saving and Giving

1. George S. Clason, *The Richest Man in Babylon*. (Penguin Books, 1955).

Chapter 17: Why Is a Faith-Filled Life Important?

1. James Dobson, *Children At Risk*, (W Publishing, 1990).

Chapter 19: Putting It All Together

1. Josh McDowell, *The Disconnected Generation*. (W Publishing, 2000).

2. John Ashcroft, *Lessons From A Father To His Son*. (Thomas Nelson Publishers, 1998).

SUGGESTED READING

The Power of a Parent's Words by H. Norman Wright, Regal Books, 1991.

Passion and Purity by Elisabeth Elliot, Fleming H. Revell, 1984.

Praying the Bible for Your Children by David and Heather Kopp, Waterbrook Press, 1999.

Children at Risk by Dr. James Dobson and Gary L. Bauer, Word Publishers, 1990.

Keeping Your Family Together When the World is Falling Apart by Dr. Kevin Leman, Focus on the Family Publishing, 1992.

Building Strong Families by Dr. William Mitchell and Michael A. Mitchell, Broadman and Holman Publishers, 1997.

Lessons from a Father to His Son by John Ashcroft, Thomas Nelson Publishers, 1998.

Celebration of Discipline by Richard J. Foster, HarperCollins, 2004.

The Blessing by Gary Smalley and John Trent, Thomas Nelson Publishers, 1986.

Parenting Isn't For Cowards by Dr. James Dobson, Word Books Publishers, 1987.

The Power of a Praying Parent by Stormie Omartian, Harvest House Publishers, 1995.

She Said Yes by Misty Bernall, Pocket Books, 1999.

The New Hide or Seek by Dr. James Dobson, Fleming H. Revell, 2001.

Raising a Modern Day Knight by Robert Lewis, Focus on the Family Publishing, 1997.

Rachel's Tears by Beth Nimmo and Darrell Scott, Thomas Nelson Publishers, 2000.

The Disconnected Generation by Josh McDowell, Word Publishers, 2000.

The New Strong Willed Child by Dr. James Dobson, Tyndale House Publishers, 2004.

You and Your Child by Charles Swindoll, W Publishing Group, 1986.

Raising Positive Kids in a Negative World by Zig Ziglar, Nelson Books, 2002.

The Five Love Languages of Children by Gary Chapman and Ross Campbell, Northfield Publishers, 1997.

How to Really Love Your Child by Ross Campbell, Cook Publications, 2004.

The New Dare to Discipline by Dr. James Dobson, Tyndale House Publishers, 1992.

Bringing Up Boys by Dr. James Dobson, Tyndale House Publishers, 2001

1-2-3 Magic by Thomas W. Phelan, Ph.D., Parent Magic Inc.,2003.
Preparing for Adolescence by Dr. James Dobson, Regal Books, 1991.

About the Author

Susan McConnell is an author, counselor and speaker whose passion is to teach principles that will encourage and promote successful living. In addition to her writing, Mrs. McConnell speaks to groups on marriage, parenting, divorce, communication, relationships, and other topics. For information about her book or speaking ministry or to share how this book has helped you, please check out her website at:

"susanbmcconnell.com"

or contact her at:

Susan B. McConnell
3750-A Airport Blvd.
PMB259
Mobile, AL 36608
Phone: (251)-342-3554

Look for her next book, *Parenting in Tough Times*, coming soon.